READY TO ROLL

HOW TO GET PAST STUCK & KEEP YOUR BUSINESS ROLLING

GEMMA LUMICISI

Praise for Gemma's first book: *Done with dull*

"This is an absolute MUST HAVE if you're looking to write copy for your website that is actually interesting! Gemma gives some great insight into how to write for your specific audience, not your general stuffy professional website that people cringe at when they read. If you're ready to be done with dull, this is the book for you!"

Natalie Brusnahan
Founder and CEO, Storybook Buyers Property Co

"No matter where you are on your business journey, *Done with dull* will help you take your copywriting to the next level.

"Gemma's unique ability to combine practical advice with stories that will make you chuckle, is enviable. Be prepared to go on a ride of self-discovery that will make you realise that everything you need is within you, you just need Gemma's help to get it out of your brain and onto the screen!

"Thanks for one of the most practical yet fun books I've ever had the pleasure of reading."

Mel Daniels
Content strategist, Meld Business Services

"For years I've struggled with business writing. That was until I discovered this book. Who knew there was an actual formula for writing good copy? I could have saved myself a lot of time and heartache had I known about *Done with dull* sooner. Not only does this book help you learn how to write good copy, but it's also a book in personal development. *Done with dull* won't disappoint."

Anna Fitzgerald
Certified Divorce Coach, Anna Fitzgerald Coaching

"*Done with dull* was the book I needed for my growing small business. And it came at the perfect time. Gemma's real-life connections to creating website copy make the topic easy but impactful. Grab your copy of *Done with dull* today.

Ashley Wolfe
Seriously Funny Life Coach, Librarian, Teacher,
Mindset Coach

"*Done with dull* is an informative and entertaining manual on how to step up and be authentically yourself in your online business space. Gemma masterfully shows us how to take that self-realisation and newfound knowledge and craft a website that is unique, honest and magnetic to the exact people we truly want to be working with."

Mikala Grosse
Tech-Savvy Business Coach, Inspired Office

"I stumbled on the *Done with dull* while searching for tips and tricks on how to write copy, because I hated to write copy for my business. Through the stories, Gemma made me see my copy from a different perspective with her specific framework that finally allowed me to put actual words on paper and not dwell and daydream about getting things done!"

Igor Vilusic

Hypnotherapist and Coach, Igor Vilusic Coaching

"Done with dull expertly blends everything you could want in a book centered on website copy. The writing is incredibly straightforward and accessible for all audiences, regardless of prior knowledge base. For someone who was new to the world of copy, this book provided a stable foundation and I built up from there exponentially. Likewise I can see this book being incredibly insightful for even expert copywriters as the motivational pieces are woven throughout the book so seamlessly.

"*Done with dull* didn't just contain the actionable advice that you would expect, but it also invoked a sense of self-efficacy when it came to actually putting the advice into practice. For example, Gemma emphasises this idea of being 'uniquely you' and why that in itself is an asset. I definitely consider my time and money investment into *Done with dull* to be 10x'd after reading this."

Zayne Khan

Certified Friendship Coach, Zayne Khan Coaching

"Done with dull is a great choice if you're looking for a quick read chock full of excellent content. I love that Gemma gave the reader action steps to take after each chapter so you can practise and apply the skills and strategies she teaches in her book. As a former educator, I give Gemma five stars on teaching her craft of copywriting to the rest of us.

"Done with dull gave me the freedom and permission to be boldly and authentically me, so that I can stand out in the crowd.

"Thank you, Gemma for sharing your gifts with the world."

Lisa Friend,
Educational Life Coach, Lisa Friend Coaching

Cover design by Mia Barnett

Layout by Lu Sexton

Edited by Lu Sexton & Stephanie Preston

Lumicisi, Gemma

Ready to Roll

978-0-6456521-0-9

Disclaimer

To my dad

For dedicating his entire life to work,
which allowed me the incredible life I live.

And for passing his creativity, determination and
freakishly strong upper body strength onto me.

ABOUT THE AUTHOR

Gemma Lumicisi is a copywriter, marketer, business coach, podcaster, author, yoga teacher and international English teacher based in Melbourne, Australia. Her career spans Australian media organisations, agencies and international classrooms.

She's a certified life and business coach with degrees in marketing, business advertising, plus a certificate in media planning a buying.

Gemma works with solo business owners from various walks of life. The diverse range of humans she's worked with has cemented her belief that no matter who you are, being yourself in your business and communicating that authentically in your marketing is what connects you with your clients and customers.

As a business owner, Gemma brings her stories of adventure and knowledge from around the globe into classrooms, zoom coaching sessions and her podcasts. She's a world of knowledge with a unique ability to squeeze information out of her client's brains into the compelling and persuasive copy. She's an individual who's always done life her way with a unique perspective of the world at large. She values individuality and education. She has a strong strategic and analytical thinking mind, which helps her discard the path to nowhere and always strike forward. Her superpower is listening to others and lifting them up to help them achieve and believe in themselves. She's an expert in high productivity and getting loads of high-quality shit done in short amounts of time.

When she's not working, Gemma can be found exercising, reading, learning or planning the next country to travel to. She divides her time between listening to music and watching her favourite TV series, writing, reading, gardening, cooking, spending time with her friends, chasing sunsets and stray animals and finding a beach with white sand to lie on.

You can find her at www.contentlydriven.com

CONTENTS

PREFACE

While I put the final touches on my book (like this section) from my room in Raniban, Nepal, while studying yoga teaching training, I realise how lucky we are as entrepreneurs.

It wasn't even just out of reach for our parents, grandparents and great-grandparents. As little as only ten years ago it was a faraway dream that we could work from home, let alone from anywhere in the world. But as entrepreneurs, we can work online from wherever we wish and be our own boss.

I've learnt many things throughout my life, experiences and travels. But being in Nepal, I've realised exercising as a woman is a luxury. Before my 7 am Ashtanga practical class, I leave the school at around 6 am to go for a run. I'm the only woman running. There are a few other runners I see daily. Some wave and smile at me, and some ignore me, but there are no women.

The women are busy at 6 am carrying large containers, buckets and tubs with their children to the public water taps in the town to fetch their daily water to take back to their houses.

When your basic needs are filled as a human, such as food, water, warmth and shelter, you don't have any other worries, but as humans, we create them. We can do luxurious things like exercise when we don't need to stress that we won't meet our basic human needs.

As entrepreneurs, we lead extraordinary lives, but it comes with many challenges. I know the emotional pain and struggle of running a business on your own, constantly selling and putting yourself out there to get a regular influx of clients. It's often lonely, stressful and most of all, it's not easy. If it were, everyone would be doing it.

Many want to give up, but I never let my clients give up on uncomfortable and challenging things, no matter how nasty their freak out is. Because a shitty feeling means you're on the right track. You're doing stuff that's testing you, it's not meant to be simple.

You need to know pain to feel pleasure, especially when pushing the boundary of your comfort. So keep going, welcome the growing pains and you'll find greatness.

Full disclosure, I've wanted to quit my business many times, I can't imagine there'd be an entrepreneur who hasn't, but I kept on going because I knew I'd keep inching closer to where I wanted to be.

I want the same for you.

Whatever your dreams are, a sustainable business, travel while running your business, raising a family while running your business, I want to help you get there through this book.

My book isn't for you if you want fast and ruthless. It's not one of the ridiculous business claims (from $3k a month to $97k) that are on the internet. Building a business takes dedication, tiring steps and consistency. Plus, personal determination and desire to love it so you'll keep going.

I hope my book inspires you to push through feeling stuck in your business. Let your light shine out to the world, help more clients and run your business your way.

Gemma
xxx

INTRODUCTION

One of the biggest things I've found with my coaching clients is that they want to give up and that's why I wrote this book. Please don't give up because you've got some things working against you.

Growing a business takes time.

Many business coaches overpromise and make exaggerated claims about starting, running and growing online businesses, but my approach is different. I'm talking about learning to love your business exactly where it is so you can keep going.

I cut this book down, almost by half, because I don't want you wasting time learning. I want you to be doing. This book has practical steps to follow to get unstuck and keep going in your business.

If you're an entrepreneur running an online business who feels stuck and is struggling to get to the next growth step in your business, then don't put this book down.

In my first book, *Done with dull*, I told a story about how I discovered the missing piece in my business was me, and that's when my business changed. Until I fell into the same stuckness again.

I was puzzled for so long. I knew my knowledge wasn't the problem. I'd been in business a while, I allowed myself to be me, so what the heck was it? It was my mind. I realised the problem was me. I was getting in my way. It wasn't my cat sitting on my keyboard or that client who didn't like my copy that one time and (in a fictional fairy tale in my head) ran around and told all of her business friends ... it was all me.

If you're like most entrepreneurs, you can relate to this, and you know the struggle of working under the most brutal boss you've ever had, yourself. Let's face it, most of us are nasty as rotting garbage to ourselves. But this stops now. By reading this book, you'll save buckets of time by learning how to shift past mindset blocks that keep you playing it safe in your business and wondering why you're not growing.

First of all, I want you to know you're impressive enough, you know your shit, and if you are getting in your way, you aren't alone, in fact, you're completely normal. The mindset blocks you have, everyone else has as well. I've done a lot of business coaching, I know this. We are all humans with various belief systems about stuff, and as entrepreneurs, yes, we are rebels and tough as nails, but we still have limits in our minds, and if we aren't aware of what's going on, then we can't make changes.

This book is split into two sections – thinking and doing. As an entrepreneur, you're doing all of the doing. I know that for sure, but you're putting off some of the doing, and without understanding your thinking, the doing stays stagnant. This stagnant energy is why I put the thinking section of the book first. To truly understand why you're feeling stuck and procrastinating on certain activities, you need to be aware of what's going through your mind. Once you can uncover this and your reason behind why some parts of your business feel harder than others, then some different motions will start to happen. I figured this out, and I want you and your business to grow.

I'm an author, copywriter, marketer, life and business coach, an international English teacher and – as I write this introduction from near Kathmandu in Nepal – a soon-to-be-certified 500-hour advanced yoga teacher.

I help coaches and entrepreneurs write copy for their businesses. Without copy, you won't attract clients to your business. It's an essential part of a business, yet one with the most mind blocks, which is why I help entrepreneurs write shit-excellent copy to get their ideal clients' eyeballs stuck to their phone screens.

Growing your business genuinely and honestly is what this book is about. You may not want to hear it and want the false claims way out of it, but I want the best for your business, and in a realistic way. I'm going to be truthful, the genuine and honest way means hard work and personal growth, a lot of shit you don't want to do and might feel a bit crap throughout a lot of it. But I'm here for you. My goal is to equip you with an understanding of your mind, helpful knowledge and the tools you need to set up and grow your business from the start.

When it feels too much, and you want to throw your head into a giant glass of wine and pretend nothing exists, remember your *why*. The reason why you started your business is your fuel for reconnecting with your perseverance and belief, which is where we will begin this book.

Ninety-nine percent of entrepreneurs think running a business is easy, and that they'll make massive amounts of money fast, but they've got it wrong, which is why so many give up, but if you want to get it right and keep going, then read on.

PART ONE

THINKING

CHAPTER ONE

YOUR WHY

"Help me! Help me!" are the screams going through your head because you can't say it out loud.

You can't deal anymore.

You don't wanna!

Whenever you speak with your client, Maria, she drives you up the wall. Your office is at home, so as soon as your meeting finishes, off you trot to the cupboard to grab a chocolate biscuit ... Or five.

You start eating thinking about how your friends have it so easy because money falls into their bank accounts from their employers. They don't have to sell, create funnels, do webinars, put up with Maria's shit and stress about whether this month will be a high or light revenue month.

Mmm, salt and vinegar chips ...

An hour later, you finally stop thinking about how much better everyone else's lives are. But as you munch on your chips, you realise your favourite snack goes down *waaay* better with your favourite *Will and Grace* episode.

Gosh, Maria is so annoying!

Before you know it, you've done no marketing, sales calls or business growth strategy tasks ... oh, and six days went by ...

WTF? It's your weekly meeting with Maria again?

If this story sounds familiar, it's not your favourite TV show, your snacks or Maria making you frustrated at your business. Here's the reality: business things are hard, especially in the first couple of years, so being frustrated and using coping mechanisms to distract yourself and relax are normal.

But if you remember why you put yourself into what can feel like absolute crap, why you're still at it and not back in a salary job, then you know you're sticking to this entre-preneurship thing for a reason.

Even though you want to run out the front door when it gets too hard, you haven't.

Guess what? This is where most business owners run out the door back to a salary job. But despite the hardness, you haven't canned it, and that's why you're here.

In this chapter, you'll learn a secret more priceless than one of Elizabeth Taylor's jewels about how to keep doing this entrepreneurship jazz even when Maria, a wonderfully paid-up client, won't stop giving you the shits.

WHAT A BUSINESS 'WHY' MEANS

It's not your clients, products or services. Your *why* is all about you and the secret gem that keeps you and your business going. I remember reading in my giant font primary school kiddy dictionary the word *why* means, 'for what reason or purpose?'

If you've ever spoken to me, you'll have heard me ask this instead of asking why. It sounds more fun to me. But over to you, for what reason or purpose did you start your business?

Answer it below before reading on. Your answer is the life-force behind your business and by writing it down now you will feel warm and fuzzy when reading this chapter.

For what reason or purpose did you start your business?

_____

_____

_____

_____

When your cousin's friend's dog's sister says that horrible thing about your last podcast episode, or you have two people show up to your webinar when twenty-two signed up, come back to this page and read the sentences you wrote above.

But there's more to your *why* than writing it down. There are some other parts needed to help you solidify your business credentials, characteristics and guts.

Own, define and create – these are the tools you'll use that connect you to your *why* because on the days or even weeks when Maria is the least of your problems, you need that *why* embedded in your mind to help you keep going.

Own your story

Firstly, own your story. Your story is you, your past and how you came to be where you are now, and your target audience wants to know it. Tell your story, write it and remember it because your experiences, failures, learnings and the silly things you've done throughout your life make up your business and who you are. When it comes to your business, it's about owning your story because it makes you the person you are today. Maybe you were a mess then got your shit together, and that's why you help others do it. Or were you an overworked, exhausted, burnt-out corporate human who created a business for flexibility and freedom?

Not always, but often a *why* for starting a business comes from a transformation you've had, so now you want to share what you learnt with the world. Or it's a talent you've got or an incredible idea, so you want to build it up and make it happen. Whatever your *why* is, owning your story is part of it because it makes you your fantastic, unique self. And that unique self is your business and what sells you because you're a solopreneur, and your story will connect you to your clients.

When I work through this initial business exercise with my clients, they often tell me their story isn't good enough or that no one will care.

Your people will care because business is all about connection. Your story is something you can share, put on your website or use to connect with yourself again. It's not a thesis. It's writing down some experiences from throughout your life that stand out to you, and thinking about what you learnt from them. They can be experiences that were fun, painful or challenging. It doesn't matter, but one of these events could help clients or customers because they've connected with it and want to work with you.

If you need a nudge for questions to help write your experiences so you can create your whole story, here are some prompts.

- What is the story, and what happened?

- How could this experience be the best thing that happened to you?

- How did this experience make you who you are today?

- What did you learn from it?

- How did it help you further down the track?

- How could you think about this experience in another way?

- How can you use what you have learnt to help others?

Re-use these questions as prompts for each of your experiences when writing your story. Remembering your experiences is an excellent reminder that you are a killer business owner and human who can help the people you work with. You are enough. You're not an imposter; you were born to get through business challenges and road-blocks. Your story matters.

Define your core business beliefs

Your story is the path that brought your business to life and will help strengthen your *why* in your mind. To further reinforce it, define your core business beliefs.

Your business beliefs are what you live by, who you are and how your show up as an entrepreneur. Write them down on a sticky note (like I have), put them on a wall, and remind yourself of your business beliefs daily. Doing this is an excellent way to stick by them when working with your clients and making business decisions.

To write your core beliefs, ask yourself two questions.

• What do you wish your clients knew?

• What do you hate that other people are doing in your industry?

Write three answers for each.

For example:

> I wish my clients knew that writing copy can be easy.

> I hate how people in my industry make unreasonable claims without context behind them, leading people into a false sense of how fast they can grow their business.

These core beliefs help you stay on track, stay aligned with your *why*, and stay focused on helping your clients using your methodology and in your way. Plus, they help form oodles of content for you. Keep an eye out for that in Chapter 9.

Create your business mission

You've owned and defined, which means it's time to create. Creating a business mission is the final tool to keep you connected with your *why* and is also an essential part of a business plan. More on business plans in Chapter 7.

Formally known as a mission statement, a business mission declares the purpose of your business to the world and the internet. By internet, check out Chapter 9 of my last book *Done with dull* because I advise writing your business missing on the 'About' page of your website.

If you've already created one, then revisiting your mission statement and purpose reignites your passion and gives you fuel that will spur you to keep moving forward in your business. If you haven't written one, or you want to update it then here are some questions to help you write your mission statement.

- Who are you?

- Who are you in your business?

- Why did you start your business?

- How are you helping your clients or customers?

- Where do you see your business in five years?

- Where do you see your business in twenty years?

No matter how hard your business feels, you'll remember it's all worth it when you realign with your mission.

Understanding your *why* means you will authentically connect with your clients. There isn't a drop of unconfidence that can ooze from you if you love and believe in your purpose. You'll project authenticity, passion, excitement and a truthful way of helping your clients and customers. When you radiate this energy outwards to humans, they'll flock to you like seagulls to a chip tray. Or me towards any bowl of hot chips.

You've used the above business tools to connect with yourself and your business on the deepest possible level, so it's time to learn the headspace (mindset) to be in that will keep your connection strong and master your commitment to your *why*.

Believe in you

Reconnecting to your why is everything in your business, along with patience and commitment. But without a deep belief in yourself, you would have thrown it all down the toilet.

There are days when you'll feel like you don't believe in yourself, that you can't keep going, and you suck, yet, you still manage to get stuff done. I promise you that your belief is (deep) inside you even when it doesn't feel like it.

When everything is challenging for you, and reconnecting with your *why* seems like you'd rather stab yourself in the eyeball, take a deep breath and answer the following questions.

- What's one thing I did today that helped my business?

- What have I done this week that's helped my business?

Finding the smallest task will remind you to believe in yourself and your business. You already believe in yourself because otherwise you wouldn't be reading this book about how to move past being stuck in your business. You'd be staying stuck. If you didn't write 'reading this book' as an answer to the above question, please do because learning about how to move past being stuck in your business and taking the actions to make it happen (more on this later) means you believe in yourself. Using a combination of belief and the above tools as your fuel to keep going means your commitment will pay off.

Commit yourself and keep going

Before you keep reading, I want you to commit to your *why* and show it off everywhere. Put it on your website in the footer and sprinkle it through your social media posts to ensure the world (and you) are on board with your business's purpose, and it doesn't just live inside your head.

Now you're committed to your reason for starting and running your business, it's critical to commit to it. I'm not talking about avoiding distractions when you're in work mode, which you'll read about Chapter 6. I want to introduce to you what committing to yourself (actually) is.

When you have a doctor's appointment scheduled, do you go? Or do you eat a biscuit first, watch part of your favourite TV show, clean the back of the TV you just realised is dusty and then show up to your doctor's appointment an hour and a half late?

My guess is you go to your doctor's appointment on time, show up and do what's expected of you. I'm sure you also show up to client meetings, sales calls or any business-related task involving another person.

Do the same for yourself.

Show up to your scheduled time of outreach sales calls, blog writing, strategy planning or whatever solo business task it is. Show up and commit to yourself and your business.

> "I don't feel like it."

> "I'll do it next week."

> "I don't know how."

> "Something urgent came up."

> "My cat sat on my keyboard and went to sleep."

> "Maria sucks."

Do any of these excuses sound familiar? We've all been there!

But here's the thing, by making excuses like this, you're not taking responsibility for your choices. Take responsibility for your actions because it's on you. It isn't Maria's fault, and kick (not literally) your cat off the keyboard. You choose whether to eat salt and vinegar chips or write a blog post. It's up to you. I'm urging you to commit to yourself. The more you practise committing to yourself and following through on what you said you'd do, the easier it becomes.

When the above happens, and you've landed in excuseville feeling disinterested or unmotivated, remember your *why*. This chapter is the first chapter for a reason. Just because you don't feel like it doesn't mean you can't do it. My first business coach taught me, "What you resist will persist." She wasn't wrong, so if you are committed to getting a task done, do it because it isn't going to do itself. When you don't have a micro-manager boss lurking over your shoulder checking to see if you've done everything they asked of you, it's easier not to follow through. But the more you master committing to doing what you said you would, the more you build your commitment muscles.

Say no. People will still love you

Part of committing to yourself is saying no to people and yes to yourself and your business. An excellent way to stretch your commitment muscle further is to practise staying committed to a task in your business when you said you'd do it, even if a friend or family member later asks you to see them.

Some call this sacrifice, but it's all how you look at it. If you've committed to following a plan and you stick to it, maybe you're not making a sacrifice. If you're putting something off that you enjoy for something more important to you, then I call it prioritising. You can decide what you call it, but part of being an entrepreneur is saying no to others and yes to yourself.

Make mistakes. You've got your back

Another large part of committing to yourself and taking responsibility is letting yourself makes mistakes. That may have hurt your brain, but yes, I did write LET yourself MAKE mistakes because mistakes are where you'll learn. Acknowledge the mistake, learn from it, and move forward with a different step. Mistakes are the best things you can do in your business (especially in the early stages). Mucking things up means you're doing stuff; by doing stuff, you're learning what will and won't work to grow your business, which means you'll keep moving forward. Not doing stuff isn't going to get you anywhere in your business so expect that you'll stuff some things up because you'll find it's easier to jump all-in on trying different things in your business.

If you struggle to allow yourself to make mistakes, I want you to grab the journal of your choice (or this book) and answer the following questions. They may not all apply to you but write down some answers because what comes up might surprise you.

- Are you afraid of failure? Why?

- Are you afraid of making a mistake? Why?

- What's the worst that will happen if you make a mistake in your business?

- Are you afraid of offending someone? Why?

- Are you scared of success? Why?

- Are you scared that you're missing out on something? Why?

Answering these questions will help you understand if you've got fears about making mistakes. Learning your thinking about mistakes will help you understand why you're afraid of making them. But if you embrace the idea that mistakes are helpful and figure out the worst thing that can happen if you make one, you can start making them with less fear. Because most of the time, there isn't anything that bad that will happen if you muck something up. So give it a go because you're committed to your business and have your own back.

Be patient

You're in for the long haul, so be patient.

Usain Bolt is the world's fastest 100-metre sprinter. I imagine he made a massive commitment to himself and kept going. Through all his fitness and running training and whatever else 100-metre sprinters do, I'm sure he remembered his reason for doing it, years and years of commitment, thousands of hours of training for a world record sprint at the Olympics completed in under ten seconds. I've always thought he would be a great teacher, teaching how to be patient and stay committed to yourself.

Business doesn't happen overnight, so don't expect it to. You're new at this and doing most things, if not all, by yourself, so be kind and patient because you don't yet know how long it will take to reach your business goals. But you believe in yourself, so you're going to damn well keep going until you do, no matter how long it takes.

Perhaps clients sign up with you slower than your bank account likes, but that doesn't mean stopping because what if the result you want in your business happens in the fourth year? You won't ever know the outcome if you don't stay committed. Or, what if you get ten new clients at the end of one month? You'll never know if you stopped on the 23rd of the month.

When I started my second podcast with my co-host, we had a listening audience of her dog, my cat and my mum's neighbour's friend. But we kept going, and at the end of our first year we hit 85,000 downloads. If we had stopped, that never would have happened, but we kept our commitment. No one sees your commitment to yourself and your business. It's yours, so take responsibility for it and believe in yourself. Remember to reconnect with your why when shit gets shitter (because in business, progress can feel slow) and keep going.

In this chapter, you learnt the importance of having a *why* for your business and all the bits and pieces to do in the early stages of your business. But business is a progression so stick around for the next exciting chapter because I want you to know what to expect coming up, so you'll learn the highs and lows of business and how going through the motions and emotions is completely normal.

CHAPTER TWO

THE WHEELS ON THE BUS

"It's not happening fast enough," he shrieked.

"What's not happening fast enough?" I asked.

As Chris receded back into his desk chair, his chin fell on his chest. He replied, "My business growth."

I asked, "Well, what have you done this week?"

"I felt anxious, so I was hurrying around trying to finish the copy of the email sequence for my funnel, finish the lead magnet we planned last week, plus create the ads and social posts," he told me in a dull tone.

I sat up in my chair as he told me this because it sounded so productive.

"Well, did you finish it all?" I asked.

"... Nah. I was worrying so much that it's not happening fast enough, I half-finished everything and then started doing more things hoping they would get me there."

"Well, did you finish those?" I asked.

... Silence ...

"Chris, thinking it's not happening fast enough is slowing you down," I said.

... Silence ...

When you run a solo business, you wear all the hats because you run all the parts, which means you can't delegate tasks or hide from yourself. When you can't escape yourself, you discover hidden emotions you can't avoid any more if you want to continue running your business. Business doesn't grow in a straight line; you won't see your numbers in a pretty, ascending line graph. Business months can be up and down, so business flows in more of a cycle as it goes around. And so will you. You'll go through the motions as well.

The motions you go through are in your mind (your thinking) and your body because when you think about your business, you think about *YOU* being your business. Tying yourself up in your business never ends well. When you start to think that problems in your business are you,

you'll start to avoid them by doing nothing or going off plan. Like Chris above, he thought it was not happening fast enough, so he went off plan. But at the end of the week, he hadn't finished his tasks or the new ones he started doing either. If he had stayed on plan, he would have finished what he planned to do and been further along in growing his business than not.

How you think about your business matters, which means uncovering the thoughts that block you from moving forward is priceless to your growth as a human and your business.

An excellent way to start to see what's going on in your head is to ask yourself:

1. What do I expect of myself? And why?

2. What do I expect of my business? And why?

Then think about if these expectations are yours. Did your parents or teachers expect the same from you? Answering these questions is interesting because you'll notice similarities to the answers to what you expect of yourself. Then you can see if these expectations are realistic, if you want to keep them or get rid of them. We all view ourselves and our businesses separately. When you see something through the retina of your eyes, it sends the picture to your brain, but your mind interprets the image to make sense of what it is, which means all humans can have different ideas and thoughts of the world, situations and themselves because we see everything through the lens of our own brains. Questioning your expectations is an excellent experiment to begin to understand what it is you really want in life and business.

3.   Ask your business friends their expectations.

If you want to test if your expectations are realistic, ask your business friends theirs and see where they may differ. It's an excellent way to let yourself see that people have different goals and expectations of themselves and their businesses. This exercise (with steps 1, 2 and 3) is the first step to uncovering thoughts about yourself and your business, and this information helps down the track when you're feeling stuck or avoidant in your business because you can revisit your answers and see if you're being realistic in your expectations.

... As the silence continued, I said to Chris, "Start a business if you want to learn about yourself and grow as a human. Because this is what happens. You find thought patterns that you can't hide from anymore. If you want to ignore them, you'll have to quit your business." Now, when I first work with a new client in the early years of their business, I tell them this because running and growing an online business on your own is the most challenging and rewarding adventure.

The second bit of information my clients and you must

know is that that you won't like all parts of your business ... I speak more about this in Chapter 6, but I'm telling you upfront because it's reality. When you run your own business, you can't avoid, put off or choose not to do what you don't like, otherwise your business won't move forward.

Think about other areas of life where you do stuff you don't want to because it's necessary for your health, lifestyle or recovery. Your business is no different. Not many people enjoy paying bills, but you do it because they give you a roof over your head, electricity and gas. Taxes are the same, but we pay them because we get education, healthcare and level roads to drive on. Brushing your teeth is annoying, but you want to avoid your teeth falling out. Your business is the same. Hate the admin side? You still have to do it to maintain the functionality of your business. Yes, you can outsource parts of your business you don't like, but in your first few years, you're usually operating solo.

THE CYCLE OF BUSINESS LIFE: B.U.S.I.N.E.S.S.

Running a business can be your life's largest self-development and personal growth exercise because you're learning, growing and making mistakes. You're the baby version of you walking, falling back on your bum and then getting up again. Business looks different for everyone, but if you've never done it before, you're always in the motion of discovering what works and what doesn't because you've no idea what results to expect from your effort. And when working towards the outcomes you start to discover emotions and fears that get in the way.

I call this the circle of business life because business is constantly morphing and moving. Of course, your business name and intellectual property aren't actual living organisms, but they are real and alive within society. Sometimes it feels like your business is regressing as we have large money-making months and smaller ones. However, I like to look at it as it goes around rather than backwards.

While your business moves around like a revolving door, so do your emotions. Every turn, shift and movement of your business come with your human reactions, which come from the way you think about yourself and your business. As solo entrepreneurs, we take every setback, rejection and podcast episode with four listeners as a personal attack on us.

It's not happening fast enough.

No one likes me.

I'm not good enough.

I don't know what I'm doing.

Everyone else's business is better than mine.

I can't do it right.

My clients sigh with relief when I tell them it's normal to be thinking this way about their businesses. It's not only you. Everyone goes through the motions in business.

Here's what's going on in your head. It's called the cognitive triangle. In psychology, it comes from cognitive behavioural therapy, and the triangle is your thoughts, emotions and behaviours.

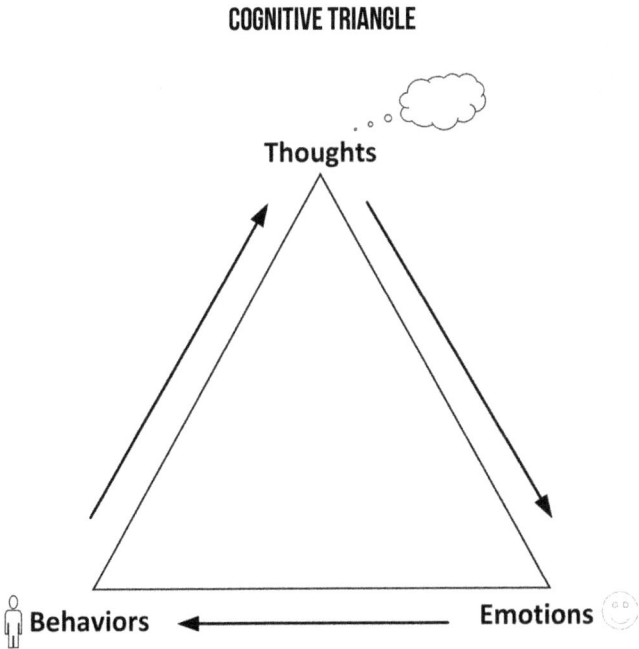

COGNITIVE TRIANGLE

Thoughts

Behaviors ← **Emotions**

Based on the idea that how you think determines how you feel and behave, this triangle is critical in business. Your thoughts, emotions and behaviours affect one another because when something (an event) happens in your business, you'll have a thought or many thoughts about it, creating an emotion or many that set off your behaviour.

For example, you have a course for your business, and you've done all the promoting and marketing tactics like emails, ads and webinars as part of the funnel. Your course goal was fifty enrolments, but you got eighteen. This is your business event and these are the facts about what happened, then you start having thoughts about the outcome of this event.

The business bullshit starts here because you can think a variation of the following thoughts:

> I'll never do this again.
>
> It wasn't a success.
>
> I failed.
>
> I wasn't good enough.
>
> No one likes me.

What happens next is these thoughts trigger many emotions such as sadness, rejection, doubt or anger, to name a few. When you're feeling emotions like this, instead of celebrating eighteen enrolments and focusing on your new students, you focus on what went wrong, which often means you don't move forward with planning the next launch. Instead, you'll begin to feel angry, dreadful and avoidant regarding your business. In this stage, you get stuck and often you can feel like you want to give up.

But I don't want you to give up.

I created the circle of business life for my business and it helped me get unstuck, so in this chapter, I'm sharing it with you.

This is the circle of business life.

Bullshit

Useless

Self-realisation

I've got this

Never give up

Endurance

Sort it out

See it happen

The business *bullshit*

I'm talking about all the thinking in your head about your business, clients and income. All the business bits you take personally. This comes from various factors like comparing then freaking out, changing things around and then doubting. For example, you check analytics on your website or socials and chuck a tanty (Australian for tantrum) because the numbers are too low or you haven't had enough email opens or podcast downloads. Then there was that one client that said that thing yesterday and now you feel like crap about yourself. All this is business bullshit, the self-talk in your head and what you make your business mean about yourself.

Useless

There are two parts here. It's useless to stay in the bullshit because it doesn't move you forward. But the more accurate U is that you'll begin to live the way you're feeling. For example, when you feel useless, you stop moving forward and avoid your business. So once you can acknowledge and realise you're in the useless stage, you can begin to shift into the next one.

Self-realisation

This is where your self-realisation begins, you are uncovering all the bullshit in your mind, and this is what you start to face and must move through to continue growing your business. The best way into self-realisation of what I call 'business-blocking thoughts' is to start to journal and see what's going on. Or speak to your entrepreneur friends and see if they've had similar business-blocking thoughts because understanding what's going on in your head means you can get it out of your head and begin to separate yourself from what's happening in your business. This is the pivotal step here and can be quite involved, so we'll look into it in-depth later.

I've got this

You've dealt with the crap you uncovered, you're working towards separating yourself from your business so you can look at your business problems objectively. Even though the event didn't meet your desired outcome, you believe that you've got this. So you begin to plan, have ideas and make things happen. Rather than staying in the non-factual business-blocking thinking, confused about or comparing what you're doing, you're sorting stuff out, and you're making things happen.

Never give up

As the wheels of the business bus go round and round, so do you. You never give up. You've reconnected with your why, and you're focused on your business mission and goals.

Endurance

This is the true grit of an entrepreneur. Even though it feels like there are endless tasks and challenges ahead, you're willing to do them because you want the business wheels to keep turning no matter how hard it feels. Here is where you shift into a beautiful business mindset because knowing you're never going to give up creates endless possibilities in your mind. You try one strategy that may not work, but you assess and try again until it feels right.

Sort it out

You're objectively sorting out your business problems, unmet outcomes and hurdles instead of looking at your business problem emotionally. So you're able to ask yourself objective questions that help move the business forward.

- What do I need to do now?

- How many clients do I need?

- What's one thing I can change to improve this?

- How can I evaluate what went well?

- What I can improve on?

See it happen

After sorting out business problems objectively, you get to watch your plan happen because you brought it to life.

So now what? Well, the wheels keep on turning and back you go to the B. Because you've sorted the current business problem out, but the next one will come. Your human self will start having new thoughts about the new strategy you're pursuing, or the event that didn't reach your goal, which brings up new problems in your mind, creating different emotions. And that is how the business wheels keep turning.

When your business grows or you do something new, awesomeness happens, but that also means you have a new set of goals, obstacles and emotions to deal with. You may leave some emotions behind, but a new set will come when you face new things. The world is binary, and as entrepreneurs we are good at thinking one way or the other, good and bad, success or failure, which means we create binary corresponding positive or negative feelings. For this reason, we must stay connected with our purpose and *why* for running our businesses because when the negative seems like it outweighs the positive (because you're hanging around B and U of the business cycle), you'll be able to see through the tough parts and remember it's all worth it.

SELF-REALISATION

Self-realisation is the pivotal step in the B.U.S.I.N.E.S.S. model so let's look at it closer. The key to this step is understanding what is going on in your extraordinary mind because it's only you who's stopping you from moving forward. When something happens in your business that didn't meet your expectations, such as not reaching a goal, here are questions to ask yourself so you can uncover what you're thinking about.

- What am I upset about?

- What factually happened?

- What are the numbers and data?

- What do I think went wrong?

- Why did this not live up to my expectation?

- What's one thing I can change to improve on and try it again?

- What worked well?

- What have I learnt?

Answering these questions means you'll discover a bunch of (business blocking) thoughts about yourself and your business. They often look like the below:

I wasn't good enough.

I didn't do enough.

I don't know enough.

I ran out of time.

They didn't like me.

I don't know how to fix it.

I failed.

It was the wrong thing to do.

I can't sell.

I can't do this.

Others are doing better than I am.

No one likes me.

It wasn't perfect.

I've had all the above thoughts, and I've heard them and more from my clients. These business-blocking thoughts then create thought obstacles because without moving over the hurdle of the thoughts you'll struggle moving forward in your business.

To get past these mental blocks, you need to do two things:

1. Remember you and your business are separate.

2. Distinguish your thoughts from the actual facts of what is happening in your business.

Your business is not you

I know it feels like you are your business because it's only you, but you're not. You are you and your business is separate, it doesn't change your worth. Nope, nope. Don't let the number of clients you have validate who you are or measure you as a person. You are separate from all of the above.

Your business is numbers, revenue, click-throughs, subscribers and downloads. The problem with business stuff and why you'll go through the thoughts, emotions and motions is that we make business numbers, revenue, click-throughs, subscribers and downloads mean something about us. Once we attach meaning about us to our business, we start to feel terrible gut-kicking feelings we don't like that come from the way we are thinking about our business.

To remind you again, you're not your business.

Distinguish the thoughts from the facts

Here are possible facts about your business:

- 348 emails were sent

- 22.2% open rate

- 4 people replied to emails

- Webinar on 5 October

- 20 attended

- Replay emails sent out

- Podcast episode had 3,800 listeners

- Goal was fifty to enrol, got 10 enrolments

Now here's what happens, when thought obstacles (like those above) get in the way of these factual business numbers: you prevent yourself from moving forward and connecting with potential clients or customers. The above are facts and numbers about your business, they don't mean anything about you, so focus on these facts and ask yourself useful questions so you can plan your next move. You can make decisions and devise strategies for a forward moving plan when you look at facts, figures and numbers. When you can't move out of the business bullshit (thought obstacles) you won't be able to create new strategies.

Once you're in objective thinking, it gives you the power to make a strategy and you're at the next step in the B.U.S.I.N.E.S.S. cycle: I've got this. Once you're in the *I've got this* mindset keep the momentum up, don't sit around and wait for motivation to happen.

DON'T WAIT FOR MOTIVATION

Knowing that business moves in a cycle is crucial because I've seen entrepreneurs go through the motions and then wait for motivation to kick in so they can action the forward moving plan they came up with. Motivation won't cast a spell on you to help you do stuff, you're responsible for moving forward and actioning your plans. This isn't easy stuff to do, which is why creating a strategy for moving forward is the key because motivation won't come and save you.

> I didn't have the motivation.

> I didn't feel like it.

> I was motivated to begin with and then it went away.

If the above sound familiar then you're blaming motivation for not doing things in your business. It's easy to have the motivation to drink water when you're thirsty and eat when you're hungry. But it's harder to have it to record your podcast every week when you've only got twelve to eighteen listeners per episode. For this reason, you can't wait for motivation.

Motivation is amazing. It's an excellent tool to get you going but it doesn't keep you going. When it comes, it's there in full force, loading you up with ideas that start you off. But it doesn't stay, so don't expect motivation to be there as a way for you to start your day, continue heading towards a goal and record your next podcast even if you don't feel motivated to do it.

As I also said at the start of this chapter, there are parts you won't like doing when it comes to business. But all bits are necessary to run and market a business, Chapter 8 covers the importance of routine and consistency to get stuff happening and competed but here I'm talking not using 'no motivation' as an excuse. Remember when you're having bullshit thoughts about your business, you don't have to let them stop you from moving forward. Once you're in strategy mode keep moving through the cycle whether you're feeling motivated or not.

In this chapter you learnt what business thought obstacles are and how to separate figures from bullshit. In the next chapter, we're moving along the cognitive triangle from thoughts into emotions, which means I'm talk about emotional business blocks ... Please don't run away!

I promise you emotions are critical for your business growth and they're not as awful or scary as they feel.

CHAPTER THREE

IT STARTS WITH MIND

In the last chapter, we looked at thoughts and how the way you think about your business makes a difference in your outcomes and reaching your goals. The next two chapters focus on the emotions that follow your thoughts about your business, its events and how they affect what you do and how you show up in your business.

Believe it or not, some emotions stop you from doing things and moving forward with your business. There is a reason for your Netflix binges, head face down in the toilet, throwing up from too much wine the night before and waking up with a fast-beating heart because you're feeling anxious in the morning. These are what I call the 'I'm growing a business' pains.

I never anticipated the amount of self-growth and realisation involved in running a business. The best part is the person you keep growing into. Over and over, you'll learn, change and grow.

Business often feels like you're in a hole digging upwards with no way out because you're not hitting your goals ... but keep digging because one day you'll find the clear sideways path that works for you. I know it sounds super metaphorical, but everyone's business is different, and we all grow at varying rates.

I deleted my entire website and domain off the face of the internet once. Let's say that wasn't a great couple of days. Thank the stars for fantastic customer service in domain companies. They're precious humans who know what they're doing, unlike me. Sometimes all it takes is one button and pressing confirm for your world to come crashing down. But it can come crashing back up, too.

But here's the thing with business. Yes, I had a mini meltdown, but I pulled my shit together because I had to problem-solve. This is what happens in business. You'll mess up and have a tantrum but get back on with moving forward. You're doing everything for the first time (if it's the first business you've run), and you learn by doing, which means you'll f-up. But the beauty of f-ups is that you understand what works, what doesn't and what attracts potential clients.

Emotions affect your decision-making, planning, and

critical and creative thinking, which means understanding your feelings can make or break your business. When you're working for someone else, you are part of a team or organisation and feel like you belong. You'll get a sense of safety in numbers. But when running your own business, you are on your own and showing your face to the internet and being alone in your mind means potential danger. When doing things solo, you'll have feelings like vulnerability, nervousness and embarrassment, and facing these emotions feels dangerous. Putting yourself out there can feel like going against everything your brain tries to protect yourself from because your human brain wants to keep you safe, not throw you into horrible situations like embarrassment, ridicule or judgment.

Did you know the world's number one fear is public speaking? People fear it more than death. If you think about it, it's because of the potential fears that you could be judged, picked on and humiliated. (More on fear in the next chapter.) It's no different from running a solo business. You are putting yourself in harm's way and showing up on the internet through your marketing, which means you open yourself up to a bunch of icky feelings.

But the best news is that these fears are nothing more than emotions, which means you can learn to let them be there, feel them in your body, and move forward.

What if a feeling couldn't hurt you?

Here's the best answer ever. Feelings can't hurt you. It feels like they can, but they can't. In business, the worst thing that will happen to you is a feeling from the outcome of an event. For example, you don't reach a financial goal for the month (the result of the event), so you feel disappointed. Or you don't hit your new client numbers for the quarter and you may feel ashamed. These emotions are the worst thing you're facing. Nothing terrible has happened, so it's possible to move forward and try again. In Chapter 2 you learnt questions that help uncover your business's blocking thoughts and thought obstacles. Knowing these sentences is key to moving forward in your business because your emotional reactions come with these thought patterns.

Remember when you went on your three-day Netflix binge, drank a bottle of wine or never tried to do that webinar thing in your business again? These behaviours are what I'm talking about. You did those things because of how you felt about your business. A business event didn't result in your desired expectations, so perhaps you think you 'failed'. So instead of moving forward, you're sitting in an emotion that comes from thinking you failed, such as anxiety, shame or disappointment, and it feels terrible. So, you partake in avoidant behaviours to run away, hide and avoid your business.

Imagine feeling the feelings but not reacting to them. Or managing your thinking more actively through channels like journalling, so you're aware of your emotions when they appear. Opposite behaviours might happen, like you'd be back the day following the event and getting on with your business activities. Not hungover, square-eyed in front of the television and avoiding your business. I call these above unhelpful business behaviours 'action loops'.

In this chapter, we'll go through the most common business thought, feeling and action loops that keep you from moving forward. The action loops are:

- Confusion and consumption spiral

- Despair and compare

- Self-doubt and flee.

CONFUSION AND CONSUMPTION SPIRAL

You're at your desk staring into your computer screen. Your mind is busy thinking about the thirty-three self-help books you want to read, recalling the seven Facebook ads you saw about copywriting, sales, niching and the 'How to Grow Your Business Without Doing Anything' webinars you have to watch. Plus, the forty-nine masterminds all your business friends belong to that you need to join and the endless lists of podcast episodes sitting on your Spotify list. Let's not even get to the 601,597 unopened emails in your inbox about the above things.

If this doesn't sound familiar, you've never run a business.

Self-help books, webinars and podcast episodes are helpful, but in moderation. When you overdo them you become confused. This is the first action loop you'll venture into. Confusion is the temptation to do things you think are beneficial. It's a sneaky bugger because you can be confused for a long time without knowing it. You think because you're unsure about what to do that joining a mastermind will help you and taking another course will benefit your business growth.

You're almost tricking your brain into thinking that learning, belonging and doing all of the above things will grow your business. Now, please don't get me wrong. Nothing is more important than learning, increasing your knowledge and understanding things more deeply. But here is where it can trap you. If you keep doing and over-doing it, you'll never do or implement what you learn.

I've seen the overconsumption consume business owners, and it can spiral. It comes from thinking, *I don't know what to do*, so you take another course or join another group, and then they end up confusing you even more, so now you truly have absolutely no idea what the hell to do next. When you consume too much, it's easy to become confused, which almost never leads to implementation. This means your next step (action loop) from feeling confused is not what you want, such as using your learning to benefit you and your clients.

There's a line between studying to implement into your business and studying instead of working in your business. Overlearning instead of working is holding you back from growing your business. What's happening here is you're feeling confused and staying confused to avoid doing hard shit in your business, and it's the most common business emotion and behaviour I see. So, it's helpful to understand where it comes from, and it starts with the following thoughts:

I'm not ready yet.

I don't know how.

I need to learn more before I do it.

Once I learn this, then I'll be confident.

It's not right yet.

It needs to be perfect.

These thoughts (and more) drive the feeling of confusion and why a spiral of consumption occurs.

Here's what to do if you're over-consuming and confusing yourself.

Step 1. Get rid of it all

Do you have printed books, papers and endless notebooks of notes you've never reread after writing them down? Clear the clutter and get rid of them. If you've never referred back to them, you won't. Ever. Give them a flick through, if there are important notes, then keep them, but ninety-eight percent of it will go. Clearing this clutter helps to keep your mind clear too.

Step 2. Constrain yourself

Having constraint is an essential part of the business. I will speak about it more in a later chapter but when it comes to learning new skills, knowledge or getting help for your business, choose one or two at the most – for example, one mastermind and a course or informative podcast.

Step 3. Give yourself time limits

Set time limits if you're getting lost in watching video after video and not working in your business. It can look like one hour consuming a helpful resource three times a week. You can do it within your lunch break, in the first hour of your day, or whenever works for you. But do it when you're alert and paying attention, and only allow yourself to do it in the timeframe you decided on and not a minute further.

Step 4. Implement what you learn

The most critical step. After you've listened, attended or watched your learning, set time aside (directly afterwards) to make a plan of implementing what you learnt, so it's not wasted. If it's not something to implement, then spend that time afterwards reflecting on what you learnt, so you're consuming and letting the information be retained in your mind for when it comes time to be useful again.

You're not growing your business if you're not using your knowledge. Learning is expanding your mind, but using it is pivotal in taking steps in your business towards growth.

DESPAIR AND COMPARE

Despair and comparison often follow the confusion/consumption loop, but this loop also occurs independently. Ever been in the middle of writing content and your mind shifts into thinking about your competitor, *I wonder if they wrote a blog like this?* Or, *I'm going to write blogs like this for inspiration.* You begin to feel a little despair, and the next thing you know, you're going backwards, burrowing a giant wombat hole with your butt (your finger clicking on a mouse in real time) and digging deep into the crevices of the other 68,000 blogs written about the same thing. Then, because you've spent so much time delving into this risky research, you believe all these different business humans are way better than you, so you begin to think that what your writing sucks.

It.

Doesn't.

Stop.

There.

What happens next? Often a circle back to complete and utter despair. Once you despair all over yourself, the brilliant idea you had for your blog disappears, and you most likely stop writing it. Why? Because you think you're not good enough, you don't know enough, or you're not ready yet to write big human blogs. You figure you're doing it wrong because theirs is so much better than yours, so you either take six million hours longer to finish than scheduled or you stop doing it all together.

Imagine what would have happened if you didn't fall into the compare and despair trap. You would have finished your blog or added to your content marketing strategy and not given two craps that other businesses are on the internet. (How dare they!) As a marketer, you will find the time and place to spy on competitors. That's when you're doing helpful research, such as looking at a competitor or doing market analysis. But it stops there. Competitor and market analysis are beneficial but comparing and despairing are detrimental.

I'm sure you've delved into the land of doing what the others are doing. But what about being *Done with dull?* (Shameless plug of my first book!) How can you stand out if you're comparing and trying to blend in? You won't be authentic if you're trying to do it like the business owner who you perceive as better and more successful than you. You risk not connecting with your ideal clients and customers when you're not being yourself and doing it your way. Your humans come to you because they want to work with you, not a pretend you or a you that sounds like all the others.

When we compare and feel despair, we can get more stuck in not doing stuff. When you're not doing stuff, you're staying stuck. Business is a balance of your knowledge and life's learnings that make your business unique. Share your wisdom in your unique way and brand voice. You have wisdom, strength and courage. Otherwise, you wouldn't have started a business, so keep on track with it.

Also, sorry to burst your bubble, but what you're helping clients with isn't original, and your potential clients have heard it before. There is no original offering, but what makes it unique is your spin on the information and your way of helping people.

Thoughts that get you into the compare and despair trap usually have the word 'right' in there.

I'm not doing it right.

I'm not saying the right thing.

My website doesn't look right.

Is what I'm doing right because that other person said the opposite thing.

Their social media is prettier than mine. ... They're doing it right.

They have more likes on their posts than me. ... They're doing it right.

They said they made $100k in four minutes. ... They're doing it right.

They're smarter than me. ... They're doing it right.

I'd better see what 'the expert' is saying. ... They're always right.

Here's the thing with being right, you can't ever know if what you're doing is right until you do it and see what happens. But doing something that could (I highly doubt) be wrong is better than NOT doing it at all.

It's about trusting you know your shit, and you'll put it out there regardless of how you feel because that's what grows your business. Each time you *don't* google what others are doing, it helps you stop comparing and builds trust in yourself.

Here are steps for you to take if despair and compare has you burrowing wombat style into the ground.

Step 1. Unfollow

If there are people you follow who you compare yourself to, there's no harm in unfollowing and unsubscribing. Remove them from your world so you can't see what they're doing.

Step 2. Avoid

Keep off social media during your business hours, so you're not being bombarded with 'grow your business' ads. Don't let the ads get to you.

Step 3. Focus

Remember where you are at in your business journey and keep your focus because everyone is different.

Have these people you're comparing yourself to been in business longer than you?

Do you know what they were doing in their early days?

Maybe (just maybe) they had despair and compare going on as well?

Perhaps they spent $90k to make $100k?

What if they're working eighty hours a week?

If you don't know the answer to these questions, or other business owners' situations, remember they were once where you are.

Step 4. Forward

The internet lies, and not everything you read on it is true. So are you even comparing yourself to the truth? Who knows. It doesn't matter what anyone else is doing or has done. Move forward with your personal business journey.

SELF-DOUBT AND FLEE

Welcome to the doubt train ... where everyone is aboard. Sorry!

Often following on from despair and comparing is when you jump on the doubt train because you think everyone is doing better and don't believe you know what you're doing anymore. Self-doubt sucks, and it's the main emotion that keeps us from ever doing anything. But I want you to do the unthinkable and welcome the feeling of self-doubt without reacting to it. Because doubt will always be your old (mean) friend that lingers around, reminding you that you can't do stuff. But you can do stuff. This emotion never goes away, so learn to understand the feeling of it, acknowledge it and let it be around but learn how to control it and not have it control you.

But if your doubt is creeping in without you being aware of it and you let it control you, then you'll stop doing stuff. Instead of working on your business, you'll get stuck by reading another book or doing another course to try and feel confident again. One of the behaviours following self-doubt is looping you back into over-consuming to feel productive. Self-doubt makes sense because if you're listening to your doubt, why would you put yourself out there if you're unsure of your ability? The simple answer is that you won't. The real kicker, though? The only person doubting your knowledge now is you inside your head, no one else.

Self-doubt is normal; as I said above, it will most likely always be there. For the trillions (not an officially counted number) of hours of client coaching I've done, I've learnt that our minds seem to love sending us into doubt, so we don't do things our mind doesn't want to do.

Self-doubt sounds different for everyone as well. My old (nasty) friend always pops back to remind me I'm not good enough, so why bother?

I'm not smart enough, so don't say anything in case you sound stupid.

No one likes me. They won't buy coaching from me.

But I discovered how to turn down the volume on the doubt playlist because that helps me get on with my business tasks and focus even though it's still kicking me (like a bomb) in the guts. Remember, as gut-kicky as doubt feels, it's an emotion. There isn't anything or anyone coming to knock down your door and get you. You're stronger than your self-doubt. If you can, let it be there and don't make it a problem. The more you let it be there but don't answer, the lighter it will get. Until it returns to karate-style kick you in the guts, but it doesn't matter if you're prepared for it to do so.

Here's the ultimate self-doubt challenge to guide you towards stopping the loop aboard the doubt train.

Step 1. Sort your to-do list

At the start of a business week, look at your to-do list and select four items from it. I want you to choose tasks that give you outcomes and move you towards business growth versus smashing out work that's easy for you.

For example, think about marketing tasks such as following up on sales calls, writings ads or posts for your scheduled webinar or becoming a podcast guest. Versus writing blogs, scheduling your social media posts or recording your podcast.

Choose four tasks that feel icky, and you've been putting off.

Step 2. Select and schedule

Then schedule times within that week to get the four tasks completed. I suggest first thing in the morning to get it out of the way for the day, but it's up to you how you schedule them. But once you've planned the time, you're committing to get it done.

Step 3. Do it anyway

Do these four tasks even if you don't feel like doing them. It sounds easier than it is but practising to feel awful gut-kicking feelings (that you've spent your whole life avoiding) while getting on with your marketing business tasks will slowly build your self-doubt resilience. The more you practise this, the easier it becomes to let self-doubt hang around while you're moving forward in your business.

Step 4. Be patient

Please be patient while working through the self-doubt challenge. It may take one week for four tasks. It may take three months to complete the four tasks, so be patient. And remember, you're not a superhuman. I hear your inner voice saying, *Speak for yourself, Gemma*, but if I don't get to be superhuman, then you don't either. So be kind to yourself. Understanding your self-doubt and not believing it is the way to move forward in your business.

By doing this self-doubt challenge, you're letting the feeling be there, but you're working while feeling it. It's a conscious way to show yourself that self-doubt doesn't have you.

In this chapter, you learnt the three most common business-blocking behaviours triggered by emotions. Next up, you'll learn what's behind these blocks and how you can overcome them.

CHAPTER FOUR

THERE ARE SCARIER THINGS THAN GHOSTS

Selling a course, and no one signs up.

Raising the price of my services.

Going live on Instagram.

Writing my website.

Asking for money.

Sounding salesy.

Getting too much business.

Making mistakes.

My business might fail.

Being successful.

Not being able to handle it.

People will say no to me.

People might see me.

My family sees my business posts

Selling on my personal Facebook page.

When I ask my clients what they're scared of regarding their business, these are some of their answers. Do any of them sound familiar to you? Perhaps you have different unease when it comes to business, but what you fear becomes the emotion driving your business blocks.

In the last chapter, we looked at self-doubt, despair and confusion. These emotions don't appear with sparkle dust through a magic wand, the cause of these feelings lurks underneath in the emotion of fear. Why are you doing more courses, reading more books and learning more? You're scared of putting yourself out there, not being ready, or you doubt your ability to give new things a go yourself. If these sound familiar, then it makes sense you may be feeling blocked in your business because when we are afraid of something, we steer clear of it.

FEAR IS THE SNEAKIEST OF ALL EMOTIONS

Imagine you're about to bungee jump, you're all harnessed in and the instructor tells you to go. Can you jump right away? Maybe or maybe not, but I bet you'd be feeling shit-scared, terror, excitement and all sorts of gut-wrenching twists inside your body. You're expected to feel varying emotions when you're in known danger. What's not openly expected is that marketing your business via Instagram Live brings up the same feeling of fear.

Here's what happens in business: because this feeling moves through your body, your instinct is to run away and hide, so you don't have to do the Instagram Live or whatever it is you're scared of. Perhaps you are scared of showing up on video and freezing, or if you do it and something happens from putting yourself out there.

Have you ever asked someone out on a date? If so, did you hesitate? Or have you never even done it at all? Doing this brings up the fear of being rejected, embarrassed or isolated. But you're not those things. Emotions don't make up your identity. What's happening is you're afraid of feeling those things. There is a difference. Yet fear of emotions is why you put the uncomfortable business things off and decide to feel 'better' emotions like doubt, confusion and overwhelm, they feel less terrible than shame, rejection or humiliation to name a few.

For entrepreneurs, fear shows up in various ways but ignoring it and not addressing it is detrimental to the growth of your business. You'll never move forward with your business if you can't work on overcoming your fears. We all view the world differently and have various things we're afraid of when it comes to our businesses. Maybe you're scared of criticism, so you never speak about your business to your friends or family. Perhaps you're fearful of being seen (more on this later), so you avoid asking to be a podcast guest, avoid networking events, or maybe you're scared of success, so you charge too low for your services or hold back on your marketing activities.

When I ask clients what they're afraid of in their business, I ask them the follow-up question, "How would that make you feel?"

Fear	Feeling
Selling a course and no one signs up	Embarrassed, failed, stupid
Raising my prices	Greedy, rejected, isolated, mean
Going live on Instagram	Embarrassed, judged, ridiculed
Writing my website	Stupid, embarrassed, judged

Asking for money	Guilty, greedy, rejected
Sounding salesy	Embarrassed, rejected, desperate, rude
Getting too much business	Shame, stupid, overwhelmed, embarrassed
Making mistakes	Failed, stupid, judged, rejected

Yuck! It's not pretty ... That's a pile of awful feelings and emotions that ANYONE would run away from.

I want to help you learn how to overcome your fears so you can put yourself out there and grow your business. This block is the key component of the thinking section of this book because understanding and moving through fear is what helps you move through the doing section of this book.

There's nothing wrong with you because you're scared of stuff.

In early human times, according to anthropologists, when we lived in small groups or packs similar to animals, we survived in fight or flight mode because our lives were about survival. You didn't have to worry about the dangers of your cousin's, friend's brother seeing you at the restaurant you weren't meant to be at on Friday night or having a difficult conversation about a pay rise with the boss you hate.

In early human times, and still for many now, fight or flight mode is how we function and what makes our decisions. We were focused on finding food and water, eating, drinking, sleeping and reproducing to survive so we could protect ourselves and our group of fellow humans from dying. We've survived so long because we are a cooperative species. We persevered, flourished and evolved in groups.

Let's think about this in the online business world. You're a solo business owner, so you are not in a group. Furthermore, the group size you are marketing to is more than a few hundred humans. It's the entirety of the internet. It makes sense there are terror-based emotions popping up in your body, wanting you to avoid doing business things that reveal yourself to the whole world just in case something bad happens.

Think about it, when your great, great, great ancestors were primitive humans, feelings like rejection, embarrassment and judgment meant potential rejection from your pack, which meant a lower survival rate. I wasn't there then, but I picture an open field, no shelter and a woolly mammoth wandering along, being able to spot you from afar without the protection and safety of numbers. Fast forward thousands of years to you and your business. You're now scared of marketing efforts because they expose you to the world and numbers of humans far more extensive than what your cave-ancestor-self prefers. These humans aren't coming to eat you, but they sure can be nasty, reject and ridicule you. This behaviour is why any type of marketing is the most common business fear. It urges us to run away so people can't see us; if they can't see us, they can't hurt us.

Your emotional business pains are valid but an obstacle to your business's growth. Like exercise, there is pain and toughness to push through, but you still do it. In your business, how many times have you pushed through the physical pains of a headache, period pain or an upset stomach but still worked moving forward in your business. You can totally do it with emotional pains as well.

LEARN YOUR BUSINESS FEARS

The problem with fear is how we respond to it. Think of the last time a giant huntsman spider appeared in your kitchen, bedroom or bathroom. If you're an Aussie reader, this has happened to you. If you're not, what insect, arachnoid or animal has popped up to you out of nowhere and frightened you? When you remember the time it happened, what did you do? Freeze, scream or run? These are usually the options of either or all, and it's the same in your business. There may not be a reason to scream, but you'll avoid and freeze. Oh, let's face it, you'll scream too!

When it comes to your business, what are you scared of? Because in your business, the fear may feel real, but (most often) there isn't a direct threat to your life. You're not in danger, and there is no genuine threat to your safety because the spider isn't coming to get you in this case. There are many acronyms for fear, and my favourite is 'fuck everything and run'. This one belongs to the spider option but not to your business.

The following steps will help you uncover your business fears and bring them to your awareness.

Step 1. Recognise what sets you off

The next time you find yourself avoiding a business task, stop and ask yourself the following questions.

- Why am I avoiding this?

- What am I afraid of?

- What am I afraid of feeling?

Let's say you are afraid of someone turning you down, which means you're afraid of feeling rejected, or maybe you're afraid of your business working, which means you're scared of feeling proud or successful. Yes, it's common to fear 'positive' emotions as much as 'negative' ones. Once you learn what you're scared of, you can look at it objectively because it's an irrational fear. By irrational, I mean that no one is running at you with a knife and you need to jump for protection ('let's not die' mode). You're scared of something that isn't a direct danger to you, which means you can learn to overcome your business fears because, yes, feelings feel real because they are, but they're not scary. They just feel crap.

Step 2. Face the feeling of fear

When you've uncovered what feelings you're afraid of, ask yourself these questions.

- Can I deal with the emotion of fear, as uncomfortable as it feels?

- Can I deal with feeling the (insert emotion)?

- Can I deal with NOT growing my business?

If you answered yes to questions one and two and no to question three, then I've got a new fear acronym (that floats around the quote spaces of the interwebs) for you: face everything and rise. If you're willing to feel emotions you've always been scared of, you'll be more inclined to dive into the deep end and do the scary shit in your business that you've been avoiding. Remember comparing yourself to others, taking new courses or writing a blog and never publishing it doesn't grow your business. You're comfortable with doing those things and distracting yourself by thinking you're being productive when you're not. Like every meme on the internet says, feel the fear and do it anyway. More on this later, but in the meantime, it's time to learn how to be uncomfortable.

GET COMFORTABLE WITH BEING UNCOMFORTABLE

Exercise is an excellent example of the willingness of being uncomfortable to grow. When you exercise, the lactic acid in your muscles screams to you, "I'm in pain, stop." (Mine speaks to me, anyways.) But you scream and groan to push through the discomfort because you have a fitness goal. Business growing pains are no different, but these pains come in an emotional form.

Before I understood what feelings do for humans, and that they're not just squidgy things inside our bodies for no reason, I would have thought "emotions grow your business" was a ridiculous statement. In a book by Eric Maisel called *Why smart people hurt*, he talks about the behaviours of intelligent people. One behaviour is that intelligent people tend to suppress their emotions because they think they get in the way of their analytical and rational thinking. When it comes to your business, I want to teach you to be aware of your emotions so you can allow for rational, analytical and strategic thinking. Understanding your emotions means you have more control over what happens next. You can't control your thoughts that produce emotions, but you can try and control what happens next. Instead of emotionally spinning and staying stuck, you can let the emotion be with you but take the hard steps forward.

One of the essential rules of copywriting is finding words that get people to feel things and do stuff. Why? Because when we feel an emotion, we behave in certain ways, such as clicking on a link, downloading a PDF or buying a thing.

Step 1. Forward plan for your emotions

You can do this by looking at other possibilities. In business, we stop doing stuff because of what we are afraid might happen. We don't even know these things will happen, but it's all the 'what ifs'. But that's what fear is, you don't know what's going to happen so you're scared but instead of focusing on all the negative what ifs, lets shift your awareness to the positive ones.

Write down the different 'positive' what ifs before doing something that feels scary in your business. For example, if your scary thoughts are floating in, such as, no one will sign up, it could fail, or people will judge me, what else could be true? People could sign up, it won't fail, people might judge you, but that's ok, or you could get new clients.

Don't skip this step because consciously writing down other possibilities reminds you that there are endless outcomes. More importantly, you've got no idea which of these outcomes will happen because you haven't even done the thing yet. Do you see how this works? Being scared of emotions you may not even have can stop you in your tracks from even trying new things to grow your business.

Step 2. The key to business growth

Uncover your avoidant business behaviours.

When you're struggling to do things in your business you don't like, don't want to do or that are challenging, and you do something else instead, what is it you do?

For example, you've got allocated time to schedule your social media marketing for the month but you put it off and find yourself sitting on the couch in the middle of your business hours. So, when you're putting of business tasks you're sitting the coach instead. Be aware of your avoidant behaviours so when you find yourself doing them you can become quickly aware and then get back to the tasks you'd like to focus on.

Step 3. Identify the feeling

Once you've identified your avoiding behaviours, you can work backwards to discover the feeling that leads to avoiding things in your business. For example, when you sat on the couch instead of returning a call to a client, perhaps you were scared they'd say no and reject you. Now you've identified an emotion: fear. Now it's in your awareness you can use it as an indicator that you may avoid something coming up but you know now it's a feeling and it won't hurt you so you can start to overcome your fear of feeling something negative and stay on track.

Step 4. Give yourself a daily challenge

In Step 3 you identified the emotions you're scared of feeling from the tasks you avoid doing. Step 4 is the daily challenge of doing one thing you hate. Only one each day, it can be the smallest of tasks but as long as it's something you're scared of doing. If possible, do it first thing to get it out of the way and then everything that follows will feel easier and the more you face your business fears the easier they will become.

I've often wondered what happened to Rachael ... if she found her pot of clients at the end of the rainbow. A client of mine, Rachael, came to a copywriting coaching session overwhelmed with emotions, teary eyed while shaming herself about her business and money. Rachael is aware of the thoughts behind these feelings but had a rough week, which turned into a spiral of feeling more crap about wasting time on her business. I said to her, "What if you had a bad week, and that's ok?" She said that helped her more than anything she'd tried the whole week. You'll also have weeks like Rachael.

Sometimes you'll be human and some emotions will stop you in your tracks, which is also ok. This emotion aware-ness work isn't meant to be there to you beat yourself up or try to work harder or faster. It's about identifying what you're afraid of due to your thoughts and then using the emotions as the identifier that you're scared of taking a particular step. But instead of engaging in your typical avoidant business behaviours, you're going to feel afraid and continue working in your business inching you closer and closer to success. Because you, like Rachael, are a badass business human.

Step 5. Face your intolerable feelings

Sit back, take a deep breath and think about Chapter 1 so you can reconnect with your *why* again. Then I want you to answer this question, how will you feel if you don't achieve your *why*?

Perhaps it's failure, shame, embarrassment or guilt to name a few intolerables. Then I want you to think about why feeling this emotion is so terrible for you by answering these questions.

- Why is it intolerable?

- Why do I want to avoid it?

- What's the worst thing that could happen to me by feeling this emotion and not ignoring or responding to it?

What you uncover will help you understand why you're afraid of feeling your intolerable emotions and open up thoughts you also have about you and your business. This exercise is a good reminder that what you're truly afraid of is an emotion in your body because you are not your emotions, you're simply a human.

Most people don't enjoy negative feelings and humans spend their time avoiding them. The exercises from this chapter could be some of the most challenging work you'll do, but what's on the other side is everything you've never been able to do because these emotions stopped you. As I said earlier, growing a business involves personal growth exploration because you uncover feelings you've spent years avoiding. But feeling them is your key to moving forward.

THE MOST COMMON BUSINESS FEAR

Ghosts don't exist! These words echoed in my head as my client Gertrude Fake Name gave me every excuse under the sun about why she couldn't bear to share her first post on Instagram. A shrill cry echoed in my head, and it was at that point I realised no one's scared of seeing something that may or may not exist. Like ghosts, entrepreneurs are terrified of being seen.

Showing up on social media is a colossal business block. You'll read more about this in Chapter 9, but if the thought of being visible makes your arm hairs stand up and a lump in your throat appears when you want to open your mouth, I want to share Gertrude Fake Name's story with you now.

She'd tell me how she couldn't figure out her first post. She thought people would think she's fake and only doing it for money or to get clients. She also believed that if she was helping people, she couldn't ask for money. On top of all of this she was doubting her ability to run her business, feeling selfish and obnoxious.

However, through our business coaching, we'd planned that a social media strategy would be part of her business growth strategy, so I was determined to help her shift past these blocks. She wanted to show up on video with a combination of still images on Instagram, so we made a goal for one video.

They say there's a first time for everything. I eagerly checked my feed daily, but the video never appeared. Gertrude Fake Name told me what had happened in our next coaching session. She made a long script, recorded herself several times, and then watched it back but never posted one video. I asked her why she said, "That's how I've always done things. It's the only way I can do stuff well, and I'm not the type to do it on the fly." When I asked her why, she said she was not smart enough to do that.

Paying attention to everything she told me, we uncovered her mindset blocks and the stalling techniques she never knew she used to prevent herself from showing up online. Together we worked through these, and we slowly got her showing up on social media. Here is part of the strategy we went through:

- Get comfortable with being uncomfortable.

- What if she could give it a crack and see what happens?

- Prepare for the worst-case scenario. Write down the worst things that could happen when posting a video.

- Conduct a mini-assessment after sharing a video with questions like, did any of the worst-case scenarios happen? Did anyone notice what you thought they would?

- Then we moved through her mindset block about 'that's how she's always done it' because trying something new is the key to moving forward, and if she's always done it that way, she won't ever create something different.

Gertrude Fake Name is like every client ever, so if part or all of her story makes sense to you, you are every entre-preneur ever because the most common business fear I've seen is visibility, especially for female entrepreneurs.

The fear of being seen plagues entrepreneurs into hiding, avoiding and feeling like giving up. It's common to have many thoughts about your business like, *It's too hard*, *it's a waste of time*, *I'm spending money but not making it*, *I hate it*, and, *I'm not cut out for business*. To be visible takes facing emotions like feeling exposed, open and vulnerable, which feel terrible because, on the other side of them, you could get more terrible emotions like embarrassment, criticism and rejection.

It is possible to show up, be visible and market your business, and the first step (much like self-doubt) is understanding that no matter what, you're always going to have a fear of some sort. Fear won't go away but you can learn to bring it along for the ride with you.

Much like the steps above, if you identified your fears and they are visibility fears, I want you to break them down into smaller tasks and do those smaller tasks that lead you towards the scary visibility task in your business.

For example, if you want to feature on podcasts, start with the step of researching relevant podcasts, next research who to contact, writing reach-out emails, sending the emails and following up on the emails. You can spread these tasks out each day over five weeks, do them all in one week. You can design what it looks like for you, but one small step each day that pushes you towards reducing the fear of being visible takes you one step closer to growing your business.

In this chapter you've learnt steps to help move you out of being stuck and lead you to ones that grow your business. However, now you're learning to be a badass fear-feeling business human, you may have hiccups like procrastination appear, so in the next chapter get ready to learn how to tackle the monstrosity of business stalling tactics that are procrastination.

CHAPTER FIVE

1,001 WAYS TO NOT DO STUFF

If you think you don't procrastinate, I want you to come into this chapter with an open mind because procrastination is an adhesive bugger. It clutches onto you in the sneakiest of ways, especially in business, because it's easy to trick yourself into thinking you're doing stuff.

Joanna Not Real Name, pencil behind her ear, leaning back in her chair staring into her webcam at me, does everything she can to avoid getting started writing copy. She hates it so much that she told me she'd prefer a pap smear. She avoids copywriting until she can't anymore and tells me that she loves getting it done last minute. At the end of our session, she assures me she'll send the first draft of her sales page before our next coaching session.

The following coaching session was the day my head exploded.

Joanna said when it came to the last minute, she had to shift it because she was too busy and had too many other 'more important' tasks on her calendar to get done. She assures me she'll do it this week.

Something shocking happened as I lifted my laptop screen to begin our third coaching session. She told me that what she started to write wasn't good, so she changed the first paragraph three times and then had something else to do.

I lied to you for the thrill of this story. This information isn't shocking at all, but exactly what I expected.

The air turned icy cold in my office and I shivered as I waited in anticipation in session four, but the shivers continued because Joanna told me she hadn't written her sales page.

If you can relate to Joanna, then this chapter is for you.

In this chapter, you'll learn what procrastination is, why you have it and why you do it. Plus, you'll discover all the ways you can procrastinate in your business. Knowing the types of sneaky procrastination techniques is helpful, because you can identify which ones you do and learn how to overcome them.

WHAT IS PROCRASTINATION?

Many people think procrastination sounds like:

I don't wanna.

It's too hard.

I'll start tomorrow.

I don't feel like it right now.

I don't have the energy.

I could smack you in the face as I throw a dictionary definition at you but I'm sure you know procrastination means putting stuff off. It can sound like the above excuses, but I'm talking about the sneaky business procrastination thoughts you're unaware of:

I'll write another blog this week.

I'm going to read the book about how to do the thing.

I need to fix the first paragraph of the third section of my website homepage.

This shade of blue isn't right on my Canva image.

I've had a better idea.

I've got so many other things to do first.

I've planned more time for a strategy session.

I'm going to record and post another Instagram video.

Does any of this sound familiar? Procrastination is putting off the hard shit in your business. And it's sneaky because most of the above feels necessary, but it doesn't grow your business or get more clients. If you procrastinate, you're not lazy, much of the time you're productive, but you're focusing on less urgent tasks that are enjoyable and not as tricky.

My procrastination style used to be doing so many tasks at warp speed, but my most complex and big projects got shoved to the last minute, so I completed them under pressure. And each day leading up to when I had to do the tough stuff, I would be so busy that I'd feel too over-whelmed and I'd push the project to the next day. But all that night (because I'm the opposite of lazy), I'd beat myself up for not getting that part of the project done that day. Then I'd rinse and repeat.

The above exemplifies how procrastination can also lead to high stress, anxiety, guilt and pressure. Beating yourself up for not doing what you said you would – wasting time with what you think is essential, so you're left with a smaller amount of time to finish the more critical and complex task, which means you work under unnecessarily high levels of stress and pressure.

You can learn to avoid most of this. But first, I want to show you the forms that procrastination appears as so you don't have to keep sitting on the train to procrastination-land. I promise, slowly, you can get off at the next stop and get shit done in your business. Stuff that is REALLY doing stuff.

THE MOST COMMON WAYS YOU CAN PROCRASTINATE

Perfectionism

"It's not right yet."

Oh. My. Nope!

This sentence is the most common I hear from clients who have a need for things to be perfect before they do anything. Which means they kind of do nothing.

I've seen clients fixate on the perfect shade of blue to use on their website. They can't hit send on an email because the words aren't right yet. They tell me they could write it better, say it better or do it better so they don't do it at all.

But there is no perfect shade of blue for your website. You won't know if the words are 'right' if you don't hit send. And you can always write it better, say it better or do it better, but does that matter? What if it's excellent how it is?

I promise you, there is no perfect anything.

What's the perfect blog? Podcast episode? Sales call or email? There isn't one. If you keep waiting to make something better or perfect, you'll never finish it. There is no such thing as perfect in business. Whatever marketing strategy you're trying out, blog you're writing or podcast episode you're recording is excellent the way that it is. Look, it may never be your dream blog, video or website, but you've got to get it out into the world and get potential clients seeing it. Perfect gets you nowhere, but *completed* is what grows your business. As long as your blog, post or website is out in the world of the internets it's serving its purpose, regardless of the shade of blue.

Perfectionism feels helpful, but all it does is get you over to being friends with Uncle Procrastination. Perfectionism is good in ways because you work longer, harder and put your highest standards into everything. But it slows down your progress, adds unnecessary time and stress to your business and limits your ability to produce more.

Guess what?

The layout of my website annoys me. I love my colours and

branding, however, my mind loves to tell me that it looks crap (as much as people compliment me on it). Maybe it's because I've looked at it over six hundred million times (probably an accurate number). However, I self-taught, designed and created it mostly myself, so does it look perfect? Nope. But do you know what my website is?

Completed.

The copy does what it's meant to, it's on brand and my clients love it. I could have wasted time on the parts I think 'could look better', but what for? It's not a productive use of my time. There are other tasks I can do in my business that take priority and move the needle forward, and let's not forget the most important things, like having more personal time as well.

If you don't strive for perfection but instead strive for completion, it could change everything in your business. Perfectionism is a killer of dreams and a crusher of even getting started because when you try to be excellent at something it becomes too much and extremely pressuring, so you can end up doing nothing at all. Well, apart from procrastinating.

How can you move out of perfectionism? First of all, I invite you to consider that there is no perfect. And if there is, then who is the person who decides what perfect is? Imagine some thinking music going off in the background while you stew over that one.

Second, there is a reason you're holding back from finishing or even starting what you're doing. We can gain something from doing other tasks and putting off challenging business ones. For example, you may be putting off making sales calls because they feel uncomfortable for you, but instead you are heavily building up your content marketing strategy by writing ten blogs. You are gaining an advantage for your business but missing out on a more direct way of getting a new client.

Consider what aspects of your business you're applying perfectionism to because it's often not all areas. You might be good at smashing out your admin tasks, but you put off recording your podcast because the scripts aren't perfect. So, write down what areas of your business and tasks you procrastinate in, and then answer these questions:

- What am I avoiding?

- What am I gaining by putting off these tasks?

- What is (perfectionism) stopping me from doing?

- What is (perfectionism) preventing me from getting?

Answering these questions will help you understand what you're avoiding doing, why and what you might be missing out on by completing other easier business tasks.

If perfectionism isn't your hindering procrastination

tactic, then perhaps you can relate to the next common one, overthinking.

Overthinking

I want to make the right decision.

How many times does that sentence go through your head? If you're like most business owners, then I'm sure you overthink. We've all done it, but it's when you're doing more thinking than doing that it becomes procrastination.

You're working hard, but all the hard work is happening inside your head. Much like perfectionism, it feels helpful, but it's not. If you're overthinking how to take the first step to do something in your business because you want to make the 'right' decision, you'll never know if it's the right decision because you'll never do it. Overthinking is what I call a lousy business behaviour. It's also when you frequently change your mind and do something different without properly giving what you were doing a go. Or you keep thinking about something over and over, which leads to catastrophising and never doing anything outside of your head.

I love thinking too. Does the idea of sitting around all day coming up with ideas sound amazing? It does to me, so I get it. But since the days of Socrates and Aristotle, there isn't a sustainable living to be made by standing around and thinking. So let's come back to reality (plus four thousand years) and learn how to stop the overthinking trap.

If you have a business decision to make, like selecting which email marketing platform to use, and you've taken residency in overthinking-land because the choices appear endless, give yourself a time limit to make the decision. For example, give yourself two hours. One to research and select your top six options, the next half hour to narrow it down to two and then the final time to choose one.

In the end, does it matter? I'll let you decide.

One mistake I see business owners make is being scared to decide because they think they can't unmake their decision. Here's the truth, you can make a different decision if you're unhappy with the email marketing platform you chose after a month of using it. You get to decide, and then you get to make a different decision again if you want to. Business is about doing, and spending too much time in your head wastes time and energy.

"It's better to have tried and failed than never to have tried at all."

Try this saying on for size and see how it feels.

Check the time as you're reading this book, perhaps its 9 pm or 8 am, either way you've made twenty (if not more) decisions already today. When your alarm went off this morning, did you decide to turn it off? Or roll over? Or have ten more minutes in bed? Or get up? That's a lot of choices before you've even opened your eyes.

You make decisions quickly in the morning, so what's the difference between those and the decisions you make in your business?

There isn't a difference. You can make a business decision quickly, do it, evaluate its outcome and make a different decision if needed. Business is about keeping those wheels turning. You're not un-making a decision, you're making a new one based on the outcome of what happened with the last decision.

If you're one to make up fictional stories in your head about all the terrible things that will happen (without any evidence to base them on), it's a time suck, and you'll procrastinate your way into never taking action outside of your mind. If you overthink because you don't want to make a decision, ask yourself these questions.

- What if there are no wrong decisions? If there aren't, what happens then?

- If you made the wrong decision, how would you know?

- What if business is as simple as a series of decisions, actions and evaluations?

There are no right or wrong answers to these three questions, but don't ask your mates for the answers. Only you can answer them in a way that feels right for you.

All decisions have potential outcomes and consequences. If the decision doesn't match your desired outcome, sit down, evaluate and make a new decision. You're human. You'll make mistakes and errors; it's how we learn and grow.

How many (adult) times have you gone to put food in your mouth with a fork but you miss your mouth? Or is it just me who misses her mouth more than an adult should? Think of how often you've used a fork but still miss your mouth, it's a reminder that even experts, professionals and people who have done something so many times, can still make a mistake. So, trying and doing is the aim of business instead of thinking and not doing.

Don't confuse visualisation with overthinking

Visualisation in business is helpful. It gives you a direction, a goal and a plan. As humans, we're lucky to have brains that can plan, think and look into the future. However, we also use it against ourselves because if we can do this, we can use our beautiful imaginations to invent negative thoughts and scenarios that create fictional fear.

The human brain is wired to look out for danger, which is why our imaginations often sway that way. Yes, all the terrible things could happen but what about all the beautiful things that could also happen? Imagine using over-thinking as your superpower to think, plan and strategise solutions that result in actual business outcomes.

Going back to the email marketing software example, if you spent a week thinking about which one to choose, think of what you've missed out on doing instead. Deciding within that week, you could have learnt how to use the platform, created an email nurture series and sent out emails. You would have moved forward in your business with an outcome to evaluate. But if you spent that week over-thinking and not doing anything, then what's the result? Nothing.

All-or-nothing thinking

Business is never all or nothing. I'm talking about the 'I'll try again tomorrow' way to procrastinate.

Patricia Fictional Name and I were working on a morning routine because she wanted some personal time before her business day. Her goal was to be up by 6 am every day to prove to herself and change her belief that she's not a morning person. We had strategies to help her get out of bed and stick to the plan.

What went wrong?

If it was 6:05 am and she was still in bed, she'd roll over and try again tomorrow. But tomorrow, the same thing will happen, and again and again. She wasn't looking at all the possibilities between being up after 6 am as practice. She thought by 6:05 am she's buggered it all up and it was over, instead of getting up at 6:05 am and calling that a massive win.

Business takes time and patience. If you've planned to do something at 9 am and haven't started at 9:10 am, don't let the 'I'll try again tomorrow' happen. Start at 9:10 and give it a go.

Maybe you get half of that task done. But a step takes you forward. The 'I'll do it tomorrow' keeps you procrastinating. All or nothing bounces off perfectionism because your brain goes straight to this or that. What you did was good or bad, it was a success or failure, and you're either perfect or a hot mess.

Much of the world is binary, hot and cold, good and evil, happy and sad, so, commonly, our brains think the same way with everything. But business is different and so is everything else. Because is it only hot or cold? Or is it cool, chilly, freezing, crisp, blistering, balmy, scorching and warm?

If you've completed a webinar and your binary business thinking goes to 'it went either good or bad' it blocks you from looking at the potential (heaps of) possibilities between good, bad and evaluation. By not allowing yourself to see the options in between, you'll keep putting off trying it again or you may never try it again.

If you're an all-or-nothing thinker, here are tips on seeing other options so you can move out of procrastination-land.

1. Introduce the word 'and' into your vocabulary instead of 'or'

I have to do it at 9 am **or** *I'm bad at following my schedule.*
I can do some now **and** *the rest tomorrow.*

The email has to be longer **or** *I can't send it.*
The email doesn't have to be longer **and** *I can send it now.*

I have to send the email by 4 pm today **or** *I've failed.*
I have to get all my tasks done today **and** *if I don't, that's ok.*

It has to be correct **or** *it won't work.*
It has to be correct **and** *I won't know if I don't finish it.*

A few tweaks to a sentence and replacing **or** with **and** can create a large shift in what you produce in your business.

2. You love to speak with a bunch of superlatives (the highest or lowest of something for the non-grammar nerds)

Pay attention to your vocabulary and see how many super-latives you use during your working days.

That was the worst.

That's the best.

It's the most I could do.

It was the highest ...

It was the lowest, the slowest or the fastest ...

You wrote a post on Instagram and no one commented: "I'm the worst copywriter."

You're learning how to use webinar software: "I'm the slowest learner."

You're creating an email funnel: "Urgh! This is the hardest thing to do."

If these sentences sound familiar, pay attention to the superlatives you use because after you think something like, *I'm the worst copywriter*, or, *This is the hardest thing ever*, you're going to put off finishing it or doing it again. This is why all-or-nothing thinking (much like perfectionism) leads you into one of the 1,001 ways not to do stuff.

When you think of sentences with these superlatives, ask yourself, "What else could be true?" and let your mind go wild because in business it's never to the highest degree, there are always other options.

3. You ignore the good parts

I was helping Tracey Pretend Name with her email list, sorting, growing and nurturing her subscribers. She decided to run her first webinar, and marketing it to her list was one of the strategies. We had a goal of twenty people to attend, but five came to the webinar and only two stayed until the end. It was her first and she completely forgot to sell and tell her attendees about what she had to offer as part of attending. She was devastated, and these are some of the sentences from our coaching session.

> "It didn't work, so I suck."

> "I didn't hit my goal, so I failed."

> "Only five people showed up to my webinar, so my business isn't good enough."

> "I stuffed up my words at the beginning, so everything after that was a disaster."

> "Webinars are the worst. I'm never doing that again."

Since the webinar, she kept putting off contacting the five attendees for feedback and sending a thank you message.

She sent the recording to the twenty who registered but put off following up with them, she'd already decided it was a failure and she wasn't going to try it again.

Can you relate to Tracey? Her all-or-nothing thinking has blocked her ability to see the excellent parts of the experience. She put off following up on opportunities that led from this and decided NEVER AGAIN was her only option.

All-or-nothing thinking blocks your ability to see there are five people you've made contact with, five people you can contact again to make an offer and ask for feedback because you want to improve for next time. There are fifteen who didn't attend, but fifteen new people who subscribed to your email list. It was your first webinar, and you forgot something, so what? Now you know next time what to do and not do. Do you see how procrastinating from following up has the potential for you to miss massive opportunities in your business? Dropping the all-or-nothing thinking lets you see the positives of this experience and how you can expand on them.

In this chapter, you learnt the 1,001 ways you procrastinate, and why you don't want to do stuff that's actually stuff. Plus, you've got tips and tricks to lead you out of procrastination. In the next chapter, you'll discover ways to get shit done that will take your productivity, accountability and business to the next level.

CHAPTER SIX

HOW TO AVOID DISTRACTIONS AND DO STUFF

The eyes on the painting in the hallway follow you as you walk towards your office space. You're feeling watched because at the start of the week, you allocated two hours at 9 am to write and publish your weekly blog.

It's 8:55 am. You keep imagining the eyes in the painting so you can run out the front door crying for help and ignore the fact you planned to write a blog. You enter your office and realise the need to organise the pile of books on the floor.

Sheesh! That was close. You cannot start your blog when there's an unorganised pile of crap on the floor. Then your cat walks in and gives you the shits, so you have to let it outside. Oh crap, you better quickly water the garden before you go back to your office.

Finally, you're at your desk. You better check your emails ... wait why are you scrolling Instagram now? You look up at the time. It's 9:43 am ... What the crap? You wasted 43 minutes. You kind of did stuff, but not business stuff.

Distractions are typical, especially when you are your own boss. Nothing's wrong with you for getting distracted. However, you can learn how to use your brain to work for you and not against you and minimise distractions and get business stuff done.

Oh, look, something shiny!

I'm back.

See how easy it is to get distracted? Here's what's happening: your brain wants you to do something more manageable, not the more complicated business stuff. But you're going to learn to be in control, and once your read Chapter 8 you'll also have the power of discipline on your side.

Perhaps your distraction is jumping on social media, eating a biscuit, washing the dishes, googling crap, or all of them. Distractions feel great, safe and comfortable – the same comfortableness as regular clients, a regular income and an organised office. When your business is chugging along like this, you don't need to worry too much. But you're here to build a business which means feeling uncomfortable, doing shit you don't want to do and understanding how to stop distractions so you can do the hard shit.

HERE'S WHY YOU DON'T WANT TO DO BUSINESS STUFF

Following your dreams (heading towards your *why*), sticking to plans and growing businesses take time. Often much of the time it takes isn't pleasurable or fulfilling your desires, but your beautiful human brain is running in the 'must have desire met and feel good now' motion. So, your mind distracts you with something that feels 'better' and satisfies you in the current moment.

Do you often struggle to get out of bed in the morning? Put your hands up, my friend! I mean, a bed is warm, cosy and safe. It's the human happiness cocktail. Answering your instant desires and not doing tough business is the same as not getting out of bed. Just five more minutes of the warm cosy paradise before you have to get out into the cold, have a shower and do life stuff. But you've got to do hard shit even when you don't like it because running a business is about putting your big human pants on, taking risks and doing uncomfortable things.

Here's why answering distractions is so easy: humans are conditioned to receive reward feelings (dopamine, the feel-good chemical), otherwise, we wouldn't do anything. Think about it, if eating didn't feel satisfying, would you do it? If food didn't feel so great, would people be overweight? But if we don't eat, we die, so our brain gives us a happy reward feeling to make sure we keep wanting to eat.

Here's what's more relatable to business: you enjoy doing tasks because the good feeling comes from ticking things off a list. How good does it feel to tick, highlight or cross shit off a list? Yeah, baby! Bloody amazing. This isn't a gimmick, and I didn't make this up. Dopamine is a chemical that goes through your body to make you feel good, even from ticking stuff off a list. It's a reward, so getting shit done truly does feel great. What's the problem, you ask?

The internet and the world have messed with us. The saying 'keep your eyes on the prize' relates to this because imagine achieving your huge business goal. How good will that feel? Freaking uh-mazing! But what if it took you nine months to get there? Would you want to wait nine months for a feelgood chemical hit? Nope. You want to feel good as often as you can, and unfortunately for us long-term business building and goal-setting humans, mini-reward systems come at us from the touch of a button without having to move.

Sex feels fantastic – there is porn everywhere. Shopping feels sensational – you can buy whatever you want without standing up. Hungry? – I've lost count of how many food delivery apps there are. Giving into all these desires on the spot is easy because the distraction exists instantly, and the feel-good chemical is available more often, faster and better. Dopamine comes at us at a higher, more concentrated level than natural (goal-accomplishing) dopamine. Who wants to wait nine months for an accomplishment-reward feeling that won't feel as good in its natural form? Humans who chase goals, complete lengthy projects and keep their eyes on the prize. That's who.

During my marketing degree, I learnt buying stuff triggers the same response in the human brain as cocaine. Cocaine increases the amount of dopamine in the brain's reward system. Which means they both feel damn great. This is why good marketing and advertising open up our needs, wants and desires, so we think we want to buy what the ad is selling us. Yep, there is psychology and neuroscience to marketing and consumer buying behaviour.

With all of the above happening in your brain, it's easy to get distracted and give in to your desire instead of doing the hard, undesirable (in the moment) business thing. But the good news is that you can learn to override this need for instant reward and get your business tasks completed, even the hard and boring ones.

TRYING TO DO SOMETHING YOU DON'T LIKE IS HARD

Staying in your instant reward space is easy because you most likely work from home. With luxuries like Netflix, coffee, Pilates at the press of a button, wine and social media, the list is endless because you've got everything you need in this happy place delivered straight to you from the distraction known as the internet.

The internet is a temptation, and the smartypants people working for the various social media and search engine organisations designed notifications to grab your attention so you turn away from what you're doing. It's like a three-year-old kid who wants you to pay attention to them doing something ridiculous, like clapping their hands, so they keep calling out your name until you turn your head.

You don't want to do stuff at the allocated time you planned (like that 9 am blog) because it feels uncomfortable, tricky or even a bit painful. Instead, in the moment, you give in to something that feels better and is more accessible because the easy thing gives you a rewarding feeling.

Your distraction may not happen at 9 am when you go to write a blog, but I want you to think about what you have on a to-do list or scheduled on your calendar, but you do something else instead. Whatever that business task is, stop and think about what your mind tells you in that moment. Here are examples from my clients when I ask them to think about why they ate a biscuit instead of writing their blog.

"I don't know how to write copy."

"I'll say something wrong."

"I'll offend someone."

"It's too hard."

"What if my cousin reads it?"

These are excuses your mind has delivered you, and if you eat the cookie, your mind wins. Remember Chapter 4 about fear. You know there is something underneath these thoughts and why you're putting off writing the blog, so expecting that excuses will pop up is the start of learning how not to let distraction win.

WHY DISTRACTION WINS

Russian phycologist Ivan Pavlov studied conditioning and, in particular, created the famous study that's come to be known as 'Pavlov's dogs'. He and his team discovered that you can condition dogs to salivate at the sound of a bell that the team rang as they presented food. Once the dogs aligned the bell with the food, they took the food away but trialled what would happen if they still rang the bell. At the sound of the bell or his assistants' footsteps, the dogs would salivate anyway. They were conditioned into a response to desire the food and still desired it even when it wasn't there.

You and I are no different to Pavlov's dogs, and distractions go further than being distracting. You see because you've let distraction win many times, you've conditioned yourself into not wanting to do hard things (aka the business things on your calendar or to-do list). Still, the same way Pavlov then unconditioned his dogs, you can recondition your brain to let distractions win much less. Because right now, you're in automatic (*I don't want to do the scary things because they feel shit*) mode.

STRATEGIES TO STOP DISTRACTIONS

At the time, hard things won't feel as fabulous as eating a biscuit or doing the fun parts of your business you're good at and enjoy, but here's what will feel unique to your reward brain. That beautiful feeling you get rushing through your body when you've accomplished something challenging.

If you still want to give in to instant desires in the moment, and if you're not convinced that distractions are interfering with your business, here's a study for you. It takes an average of 23 minutes and 15 seconds to get back to your task once distracted, according to a University of California Irvine study. Furthermore, during this study, they found that people compensated for interruptions by working faster but experienced more stress, frustration and pressure. Sounds similar to what you do when you procrastinate and push things to the last minute, right? Well, answering to distractions is another form of procrastination, so if you want to reduce your business's stress, frustration and pressures, read on.

Step 1. Notice the distraction trigger thoughts

You'll have a cue or trigger that tells you to run away from the hard business thing. The cue is always a thought, or a few thoughts, running through your head, telling you something else is way more desirable. Keep a distraction journal with you, and each time you notice you're avoiding a business task, write down what your mind is telling you about it.

Step 2. Learn the distraction actions

Once you've uncovered the trigger thoughts, it's time to figure out what your mind tells you to go and do (actions) instead so you can learn what your distractions are. Once you uncover your distraction triggers you can remove them ahead of time to keep your focus sharp on what you're doing. Grab a notebook and make it your distraction journal. Write down what it is you do instead of the business task because you can learn how to control what happens next. Instead of answering to the distraction you can acknowledge the disruptive trigger but then continue doing your business task. This method is changing what happens next and it slowly un-conditions you from answering to instant desires.

Step 3. Remove the distractions

"Oh, hang on a minute, there's a thing I want to buy. I better check it's still available online." Half an hour later, you're feeling great because your shiny new thing will arrive in a few days. Twenty-five minutes later, you're freaking out, trying to get back into what you were doing, and feeling the pressure because you're running out of time. Was it worth buying the thing?

In the book *Willpower* by psychologist Roy Baumeister, he tells us that people fight desires all day long, and the most common ones are eating, sleeping, having sex, taking a break from hard work and then a combination of checking either email, social media sites, web browsing, listening to music and watching TV.

The bad news is you've got all of these available to you but no one is watching over you to ensure you don't get distracted. Distractions are highly likely for entrepreneurs, so here are the top tips to remove as many as possible so you can remain in business working mode.

1. Never work with your phone next to you on your desk. Please put it on silent and have it in another room.

2. Don't store snacks close to your desk or in your office room.

3. Keep the orgasms for sexy time.

4. Remove email notifications from popping up on your computer screen.

5. Apart from calendar reminders, remove all types of notifications that can pop up on your computer screen.

6. Use a newsfeed blocker on your social media accounts so even if the temptation comes to open Facebook on your desktop, there will be nothing there to look at when you do.

My hyper-sensitive snake ears can hear the sound of your mind freaking out ...

But what if it's an emergency?

I'm waiting on an important email.

The kids' school might call me.

The world will wait. Your emails will stay. You don't need to reply to emails instantly, there isn't an email that can't wait until later. Missed calls can also wait until you pick up your phone. You can call 000 (911 for US readers) for the appropriate service in an emergency. If you're waiting for something important, like a call from the doctor, school or parent, then keep your phone next to you. But 98% of the time, you won't need it. People designed your phone to distract you, but you don't have to let it.

Create time in your business working day for checking emails and other admin bits and pieces. But when you're in working mode, you're in it and nothing else. You decide the priority of your work in your business and what comes first for you.

Finishing your task uninterrupted or answering an email, the choice is yours.

Step 4. Expect not to want to do it

I met Lana when she was thirty-six, but when she was thirty-one she bought a domain name and registered a business. She's now thirty-six and repaid her business registration to hold it for another five years because she still hasn't started it. She loves ideas, her mind wanders away with the clouds, and she gets excited to try and create new things. Super excited with as much love and energy as a cat being fed, she gets ready to hit the ground running, make a plan and implement it. But then Lana doesn't want to do it anymore because she doesn't know where to start, and it's just too hard. When she goes to do it, her trigger thoughts come at her like a bullet with, *I don't wanna*, *I don't know how*, and *It's too hard*.

I told Lana this is entirely normal because her mind doesn't want to do hard things, so the key for her is planning and creating strategies. And her first strategy is knowing that she's not going to want to plan or do the plan. She found this liberating to hear because instead of fighting the resistance and feeling guilty all the time for not doing anything, she could accept that not wanting to do the hard thing is normal. So together we worked backwards. I took her through creating strategies to stop her distractions and then we created a business plan for her step-by-step so she could finally get her business up and running. Expecting to not want to do it meant she was able to acknowledge that but get on with it anyway with her *why* in the forefront of her mind.

You've uncovered your thoughts and what you do when distracted, then learnt how to get rid of all your distractions. Now it's time to consider knowing, like Lana, you won't want to do the (tricky business) thing because you know your mind wants you to chase and find something that feels better. But you're a big business human now, so you're not going to listen to those sentences running through your mind because, regardless, you're slowly conditioning your mind not to answer to desires while in business working mode.

Step 5. Reward yourself

Focus on your future feeling, not how you're feeling now, because you're learning not to give in to your current feeling of desire. Like ticking off your to-do list, imagine completing everything on your schedule, calendar, or list daily and giving yourself complete guilt-free relaxation, fun or even more sexy time, instead of feeling guilty because you didn't get all of your business things done. When you're feeling guilty for not completing something, what happens? You'll drink wine, stare at Netflix for too long and scroll Instagram for five hours thinking about all the stuff you didn't achieve today. You're not being present for any part of it.

What if you could get your shit done and then reward yourself? Because you can still drink, binge Netflix, online shop, watch Instagram and engage with the person sitting next to you but do it all guilt and thought-free. By the way, it feels so much better this way – the dopamine hit after getting all your business goals and tasks done feels amazing. Then you get to indulge in as many intensive dopamine hits as you want, baby!

Here's how to achieve getting shit done and then rewarding yourself. Play around with a scheduling method that works for you. Do you work in smaller chunks of time? Perhaps one hour and then a ten-minute walk around the block and back to one hour. Or do you prefer a massive piece of time, like three hours, a two-hour break and three hours again? Trial and error what works for you, but give yourself a mini-reward when you've completed what was on your calendar or schedule. Your brain works on doing things and getting rewards, so take advantage of it.

When planning significant business goals or projects, break them down into smaller tasks so each feels more achievable. This way, you get a brain a chemical reward after each, whether it's one task a week over a year or one a day over a week. It all works the same to keep you on track towards that goal and get more minor hits of rewards rather than letting the distraction feel-good hit take over.

Get your business shit done first and play later.

During your trial-and-error times and following these strategies, please let it take all the time it needs. Some people may be able to eliminate giving into distractions in a week, month or some a year. The distractions will take over but don't beat yourself up if they do because you're learning to override something that's hard to change. You're asking yourself to do something challenging and maybe boring over something fun and pleasurable. But keep focused on your *why* and follow the plan to learn how to stop your distractions.

In the next chapter, you'll discover how to plan your business correctly (from the start), so you can keep focused and move forward, while practising techniques from this chapter and the last to help keep you on track.

PART TWO

DOING

CHAPTER SEVEN

FAILING TO PLAN IS PLANNING TO FAIL

Do you have heaps of fantastic business ideas that never leave your brain? Or maybe you write them down and think about implementing them but never do.

I get it.

You get excited with ways to help your clients but then imagine how long it will take to organise the ideas, so the excitement dwindles until you push the ideas away to the back of your mind and never bring them to life.

What if they could happen?

They can. You've just skipped the most important part, the plan. Without a plan, you'll never stay on track, complete tasks or give new ideas a go. You'll find excuses for not getting things done, plus no experimentation or measurement of your marketing.

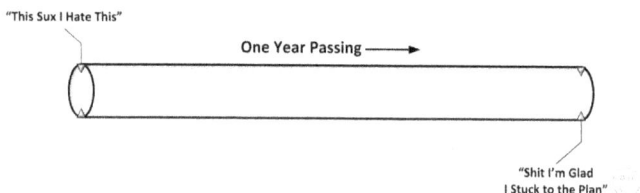

The arrow shows the plan you stuck to when stuff got hard. Even though you started at, *This sucks,* you kept going according to plan, through the thought obstacles all the way to, *Shit, I'm glad I stuck to the plan.* When marketing gets tough without a plan, you'll stay close to, *This sucks*, which is why you create a strategy and stick to the plan.

Don't be a haphazard business owner because disorganisation won't get you far – more on this in the next chapter. Creating a plan, especially for your marketing, means you're following steps, putting yourself out there and getting an outcome. Without structured outcomes, you can't get analytics or data back, which is your tool for measuring what's working and not working in your business.

The other important reason to follow plans is to prevent

you from constantly changing your mind and trying something different. Changing your mind a lot means not giving your marketing enough time to gain some traction to be able to track the outcomes. You're jumping to try something different immediately without giving it a reasonable testing period, which will never give you thorough information about your target market and the market environment. Instead, create a plan, stick to it and gather sufficient data from testing the market before you change your mind and try something different. This method is far more effective for growing your business and prevents switching and confusing your target audience with inconsistency, an overload of lead magnets or products and mixed messaging.

THE TALE OF WEBINARS TO NO ONE ...

As entrepreneurs, we all have a version of the story of The Webinar to No One. I've got a few versions. They're lonely and crappy tales but also stories of perseverance and belief.

It was a gloomy Melbourne July evening, and the clock was about to strike 7 pm. Sitting on my desk chair, chirpy yet squirmy, my smile beaming from ear to ear because I had perfected the set-up of my webcam, microphone and whiteboard.

I was eager to start my first-ever webinar. I'd done everything 'right'. I used Facebook ads as the marketing tool, and the ads did well. I received new email contacts that built up my list. I had a high click-through rate for my ads and a high conversion rate for my landing page.

And then ...

No one showed up ...

The time was 7:21 pm as I struggled to continue holding my fake smile beaming from ear to ear while still blabbering about the art of copywriting in business.

My eyes repeatedly looked at the red recording symbol, so I could stop looking at myself. As crap as all this felt, I still finished the webinar to no one.

What would you do if you knew the exact future date your marketing degree would fail you?

It didn't. I'll stop being dramatic.

But at the end of your first webinar to no one it sure feels that way. Once I had the recording, I emailed it to the list of no-shows.

Can you guess what happened next?

All up in my business bullshit head, I didn't stick to my plan – the plan of holding eight webinars, each reflecting the modules in my copywriting course. Instead, I stopped. I never followed up with my email list after sending the recording. I never followed up, asking for feedback about the recording or on why these people never showed up. Was it the wrong time? Did I not send out enough reminders? Was the landing page confusing? It could be all of these things or none of them. I wouldn't know because I never asked.

I gathered no information to improve for next time. Following up meant I could have made different decisions for my next webinar, got my marketing more precise and tweaked my next round of ads, which means the next webinar would have had a higher chance of having more than zero attendees.

Don't make this mistake.

Don't do marketing stuff in your business and run away because you didn't get the desired result. Decide a plan for your upcoming business marketing activities and see it through. I've done webinars to no one since this tale. But guess what happens? You get feedback and information to tweak the marketing for the next one. And the next one and the one after that until people start coming, clients start converting and the marketing becomes on point. If I stopped at the first workshop to no one? I wouldn't have had any of the business growth since. Hence this tale is one also of perseverance and belief.

Webinars to no one are a part of leading you towards your business vision. I'm not just talking about monthly or yearly goals. I'm talking about your overall master plan, a business plan. A business plan is the first step in your entire business. It helps you stay on track so you can work towards your vision. Yet I've seen many business owners running their businesses without an initial business plan.

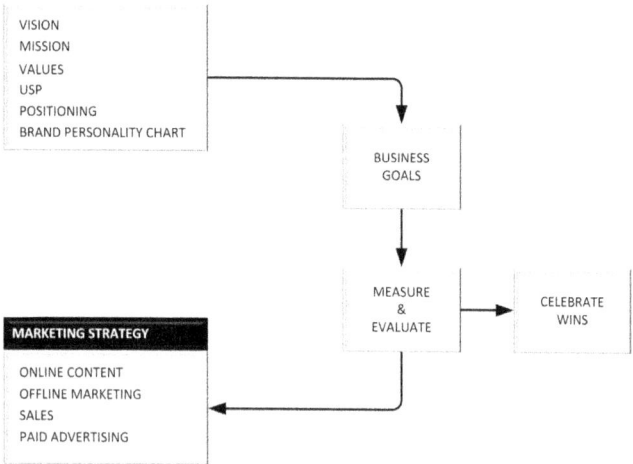

This chapter teaches you how to create a business plan so you don't get all up in the business bullshit when things don't go according to your expectations. In Chapter 1 you developed your vision and mission. These are the foundations of your business plan. Now we'll look at what else a business plan needs so we can flesh it out for you to stay on track and align your current business goals with your overall business vision.

BUSINESS PLAN

| VISION |
| MISSION |
| VALUES |
| USP |
| POSITIONING |
| BRAND PERSONALITY CHART |

BUSINESS GOALS

MEASURE & EVALUATE

CELEBRATE WINS

MARKETING STRATEGY

ONLINE CONTENT
OFFLINE MARKETING
SALES
PAID ADVERTISING

YOUR VALUES

Defining your values adds to how you want to position yourself as a business owner. Your values are what you stand by and believe in, and as a solo business owner, they're adjectives (describing words) that express you and display your personality. If you're stuck defining your values, ask your friends how they would describe you and imagine how your current clients describe you to other people.

Values can look like this:

- Dependable

- Relatable

- Authentic

- Fun

- Transformational

- Passionate

- Unique

- Pioneering

- Caring

Write down your top five values

1.

2.

3.

4.

5.

UNIQUE SELLING PROPOSITION, YOUR USP

There are six hundred thousand (not an official number) other businesses who do precisely what you do. This means it's time to define your difference and display a unique selling point.

How are you unique? What sets you apart?

I'll answer these questions for you. You are yourself. There is no one else like you. Your point of difference is using yourself as your marketing strategy.

Answer these four questions:

1. Who are you?

4. What do you do?

5. Who do you do it for?

6. Why are you different?

And then, write a couple of sentences. This is how you create your unique selling proposition. Here's an example.

> I'm Gemma. I help coaches write copy. Unlike other copywriters, I'm a certified life coach, which means I understand mindset writing blocks. I teach the one trick no one else ever has about how to write copy.

Once you've created your USP, put it at the front and centre of your website, and use it as your social media bio as well as an elevator pitch for when you meet new people.

POSITIONING

Once you define your uniqueness, it's time to set up your position in the online business world. A recognisable brand is an excellent way to add to your identity because only your business has your branding and position. Your positioning begins with how you show up on your social media platforms, with clients on video calls and in person.

Are you casual or professional? Cute or tough? However you describe yourself and show up, ensure it's authentic to you and keep it consistent with your audience. Speaking of a target audience, don't forget them when you decide on your positioning. For example, suppose your business has something to do with classical music. In that case, you may not want to show up on social media in death metal t-shirts, which will appear inconsistent with your business and won't appeal to your audience.

Outside of copywriting and coaching, I'm an avid yogi, runner, boxer and gymnastics girl. My love for words matches my passion for movement, so I mostly show up in my exercise gear in my business if it's not leopard print stuff. Ok, you got me ... it's a combination of both. However, it took me years to be ok with doing this; I had a perception that because my business is 'professional', my clothes had to reflect that. But who defines professional clothing? Does your target audience care about what you're wearing over Zoom? Mine, nope. Yours maybe, but you'll be aware of this. Either way, your best marketing strategy for business is yourself, which includes what you show up in.

If you're thinking that writing some descriptive words seems unnecessary, it's not. Defining your values comes in handy everywhere in your business. For example, you can infuse your values into your copywriting because it keeps your copy unique by dribbling a bit of 'you' in there. Let us create a brand personality chart to keep your copywriting consistent and sound like you: the next step of your business plan.

BRAND PERSONALITY CHART

This is a communication plan for you and your business about who you are and how you show up. This is a crucial part of your business plan and handy to refer to when writing copy. Adding your values that describe your personality and belief system, it's a more in-depth idea of who you are and are not.

Create a list of adjectives (describing words) that best describe you. These can be your values or different words. Then summarise these words into a sentence for what you are or aren't, in a way that best describes you.

For example:

> My business is confident yet approachable.
>
> I'm knowledgeable but accessible.
>
> I'm strategic but fun.
>
> I'm analytical but not boring.
>
> I'm cheeky but well-informed.

This chart helps keep your copy consistent and in your tone of voice. Refer to these when you're writing copy, so it always sounds like you.

If your copy is personality infused, then it can't get stolen. By stealing, I mean, let's say another business copied and pasted a blog of yours onto their website. If someone else read it, they'd know it wasn't theirs because it's not on brand and sounds too distinctively like someone else and their different brand.

Always maintain your branding and positioning. Don't change your colours after a year, write in different sounding personalities or keep updating your logo because people start to recognise you, so don't confuse them. How do you recognise McDonald's? Yellow M or arches. Coca-Cola? Red, white and black.

Once you've sorted the initial parts and core elements of your business plan, think of the initial parts at the guts or root of your business. It's time to get into the goals and how you plan to achieve them.

GOALS AND ACTION PLAN

List your goals for the year. Goals can be focused on clients, blogs, podcasts, ads or revenue. Or personal business goals like presenting at a conference. Examples include a financial goal for the year or to release thirty podcast episodes.

List your goals here.

1.

2.

3.

4.

5.

6.

7.

8.

9.

10.

When writing your goals, ensure they're measurable, otherwise you won't know if you've achieved them or not. For example, a goal like, 'I will have more confidence at the end of this business year' is impossible to measure.

After listing your goals, write them in a sentence or short paragraph like you're celebrating them in the future. It's an excellent way to visualise working on them and also helps you look forward to your business vision.

For example, if you're creating your goals for the year in January then you'd write the following:

> December 31st, and I've made $101k in my business. It's New Year's Eve. I'm with my friends on the beach with sand under my feet, celebrating reaching my goal for the year.

THE 6-MONTH MARKETING STRATEGY

Strategy is the most challenging part of your business plan. Firstly, it helps you reach the business goals you just created. Secondly, like your goals, this section gets updated regularly as your business grows and changes. Strategy is your marketing, the idea of how you'll get your business out there to get clients. Marketing is tricky, as you know, because you discover thoughts and emotions that hold you back, which is why a plan is essential to successful marketing and business growth. Here are the different sections that make up the marketing strategy section of your business plan.

Online content

Online content means business tools such as a blogs, podcasts, guest appearances, guest podcasts, sharing others' content and videos, plus, your social media strategy (more on that in Chapter 9.)

Which marketing activities will you choose? A blog and podcast? How often will each get released? If you want to be a guest on podcasts, how many appearances do you want? List all your content marketing types and precisely what you'll do.

While the content and offline marketing are part of your business growth strategy, they're more focused on making relationships to nurture clients and potential clients. Content marketing isn't sales or promotion-focused but to create awareness and exposure of your business so you can build a know, like and trust factor across various internet platforms. It's used to show you as a person and share tips and helpful advice related to your expertise.

Offline marketing

Decide if you'll do offline marketing for your business and, if so, what type. Many business owners forget there is a world outside of a computer screen and connecting locally is a crucial part of your business.

Here are some ideas to get you started:

- Exhibitions

- Council meetings

- Networking

- Business lunches

- Guest speaker events

- Handing out show bags

- Events at co-working spaces

- Collaborations with local businesses

Decide on your offline marketing efforts, how often and in what months and dates you'll do them within the six-month plan. This section is the first of your marketing plan. When you've got the months and dates sorted, it helps you stay on track and do them no matter how you're feeling. This is why the first few chapters of this book came first. Understanding business mindset helps you stay on track and follow your marketing and business plan no matter what.

Sales

The next section of your strategy is the sales strategy. These are the tools you'll use to get new clients into your business.

Examples include:

- Webinar

- 5-day challenge

- Facebook group

- Email challenge

- Workshop

- Giveaway

- Mini-course

- Training

- Discounts

- Specials

- Competition

The above strategies are known as lead magnets. A lead magnet is a free offer that gets people onto your email list because you're giving away helpful information they can use to solve a problem or a free product that they want to try. Your sales process starts with a free offer to connect your business with more people, so you've got them in your business world ready to nurture.

Then once you've connected with the new person on your email list, you'll nurture them through email marketing as a friendly and helpful way to bring them into the next part of a sales funnel which is to make a purchase off you.

The sales funnel process looks like this.

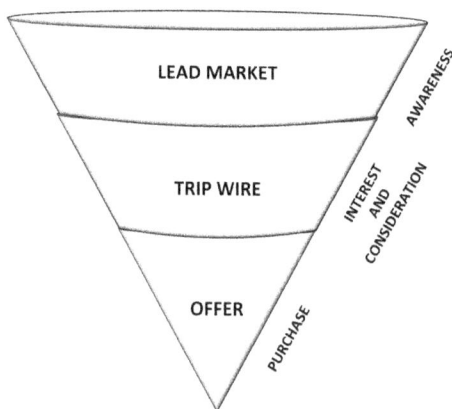

LEAD MARKET

TRIP WIRE

OFFER

AWARENESS

INTEREST AND CONSIDERATION

PURCHASE

A lead magnet is free and appealing to your target audience. Your tripwire is a way to persuade potential clients to buy something from you at a low cost. Once they've bought from you, you can develop a relationship with them to purchase your core offer and highest ticket item.

Let's say you're a business coach for new online service businesses.

- Lead magnet: free mini-course Sort Your Niche in Three Steps

- Email nurture sequence

- Trip Wire: three coaching sessions for $300 (one-time offer)

- Offer: $3,000 three-month business coaching package

Don't skip the (tripwire) middle part of your funnel because once you're working with the client, you can grow a relationship with them. Which means it's easier to sell them into your higher core offer.

Most people don't buy a high-ticket item without having proof you can help them. Smaller cost offers help grow your business and get more clients and customers into your world. If you're struggling with selling your core offer, focus on a tripwire first. A funnel is an upside-down triangle. The smallest amount of people will become your clients. Business is a numbers game. The more people you come across, the more potential customers you can create.

Imagine you've got 1,000 people on your email list, and you send two weekly emails – one with helpful tips and one with an offer. Of the 1,000, 119 bought your tripwire offer, and twenty-one of them are current clients with your high-ticket request. If your list is 10,000 instead of 1,000, you've got more people to reach out to and more people to work with you.

A key focus of your sales strategy is the lead magnet. In the awareness stage of your business you've got the largest audience and it's where you want to focus your attention so you can keep getting new people in front of your business. What can you keep offering for free that's valuable and helpful to your clients? Keep working on your lead magnet, have a few not just one and keep looking at ways to make them so appealing that people can't wait to grab them. Your lead magnets are available on your website and you direct people to them through your content marketing.

Paid advertising

Paid advertising efforts:

- Facebook ads

- Banner ads

- Website ad

- Digital magazine

- Influencer

- PR

- TV ads

- Radio ads

- Directories

- Local directories

If you're ready to drive more clients into your world, above and beyond content marketing, you can ramp it up with paid ads. Your ad is what sends people to your lead magnet or freebie.

Paid ad > Freebie > Client in your world

I could write another book on advertising (it's one of my degrees), but for now don't forget to add it to your marketing strategy (and budget for it) if you're going to pay for advertising and increase your exposure.

MEASURE FOR SANITY

In business, it can be challenging to see if your efforts are working, especially your content marketing. But there are tools available to check all these statistics. There are website analytics available for you in the back end of your website, where you can see how many people clicked on your blogs, shared or commented. This type of analytical data gives you information about what's working and not working in your business because you can see how many people are clicking on specific pages of your website or the comments you get on particular social media posts. For example, if analytics tell you that a piece of content got many likes and comments on social media, you can re-purpose, create more and use it again to keep growing that traction.

Here are excellent questions to ask when measuring your marketing:

- Is the outcome different from last time? (Whether it's last week, yesterday or the previous launch.)

- How is it different?

- What went well?

- What didn't go well?

- How can I improve?

- What are the numbers?

- Is there an increase or decrease? And why?

Measure each marketing outcome so you can move forward and keep on track.

CELEBRATE GOOD TIMES

After all of the above, don't forget the most important part, celebrate your achievements. If you don't celebrate after your wins, it's time to start straight away, otherwise you'll never be content with how things are going in your business. I've worked with business owners who make $50k a year, but all they can think about is their goal of $150k instead of stopping to celebrate the shit out of making fifty thousand dollars all by themselves, plus everything along the way because that's worth celebrating. Heck, reaching any goal you set out to achieve is worth celebrating, it doesn't matter how large or small. Celebrate your achievements, and don't forget to give yourself a reward, whatever that looks like for you.

In the next chapter, I'll teach you three ways that help get you to stick to your marketing and business plan. We've covered mindset, and you've learnt how to create a plan for all your wonderful ideas so you can bring them to life.

CHAPTER EIGHT

BUILDING BUSINESS HABITS

*"We are what we repeatedly do.
Excellence then is not an act, but a habit."*

—Will Durant

This quote is frequently misattributed to Aristotle but it appears that Will Durant was paraphrasing the ancient Greek philosopher in his 1926 book, *The Story of Philosophy.* Either way, it's a good quote.

This chapter is non-negotiable, so please don't skip it because once you master good business habits, you can do tedious business tasks (yep, the ones you hate) at warp speed. The key traits we'll cover in this chapter for you to develop as part of forming habits and staying on track in your business are discipline, routine and consistency.

Here's what this looks like:

- Discipline is your friend.

- Routine is the key to discipline.

- Planning is the key to routine.

- Consistency results from sticking to a routine.

Consistency is good for you because it helps you produce fantastic results in your business. It's also excellent because it lets you stay on track with moving forward when you (and your thoughts and emotions) are getting in your way.

If you're like most people who cringe at the thought of being disciplined, then it's time to learn how discipline is your friend, routine isn't your enemy and consistency is kind. These soon-to-be three amigos will help you develop habits in your business that assist in getting shit done.

This chapter has reasoning and practical bits for understanding why these three amigos work. Plus, you'll learn tricks to become a systematic master so you can develop habits in your business to help you get things done even when you don't feel like it.

DISCIPLINE IS YOUR FRIEND

"The first and best victory is to conquer self."

—Plato

I'm fortunate because discipline comes naturally to me, but I will teach you how to master it. One day, my best friend mentioned how she admired my discipline as an impressive strength of mine. Before this, I never thought of myself as being disciplined. I assumed it was the same for everyone. Once learning discipline is my superpower, I dug into myself and uncovered what's different about how I do things compared to others and I've been helping clients with discipline ever since.

When I finish writing this book, I'm off for six weeks of yoga training in the Himalayas in Nepal, and during this time we aren't allowed any distractions to our minds such as nicotine, caffeine, drugs and alcohol. Yes, it will take discipline, power and the universe to survive the horror of no coffee, but why not? I'm all in.

When I tell people about this adventure, the first comment is, "I could never do that."

Did you have a similar thought when I told you about it? My answer to them is, "Why?" and we enjoy a few seconds of confused gazing into each other's eyes because, as I said, discipline comes easy to me but not most.

Throughout this book, you've learnt about business growing pains, like feeling unsettling emotions and facing your fears. Discipline helps you stay on track when you're feeling uncomfortable because staying in the uncomfortable is what grows your business. I'd like you to challenge yourself to form discipline in your business, which pays off. Because the rest of your hours are free to be as undisciplined as you please.

There are many quotes I could throw at you, like 'Short-term pain for long-term gain' or 'You can't have success without sacrifice'. Remember I spoke about sacrifice earlier? Like many business owners, you probably find it's easier to show up for other people like your clients than for yourself.

Discipline helps you master commitment to yourself, which builds on from Chapter 1. I think of discipline as personal management, inner strength and self-control. Mastering this level of inner strength means always doing what you say you will, not giving into desires and thinking beyond basic human needs. The more you can keep commitments to yourself, the more accessible discipline becomes. When I say I'm going to do something, I do it, no matter how I feel. It sounds simple, but it can be challenging if you're new to the world of discipline, but it gets easier because, after a while, you don't think about it. You simply do it.

What's interesting about discipline is you'll get more done, be happier (remember those dopamine hits?) and feel more satisfied in your life and business. The same goes for the parts of your business you don't like. Use discipline to get you through the discomfort of doing things you don't want to do.

Discipline increases your chances of success because you're focused. It helps you keep on track while you move towards your business vision. When you're growing your business and doing the same things over and over to get clients, it's challenging to keep aligned with your vision.

Picture this. You're driving a car, but you keep looking at what's behind you in the review mirror because you're worried about someone coming up too close. Eventually, you completely take your eyes off what's in front of the vehicle so you can keep staring into that mirror.

What happens next?

CRASH.

You'll eventually crash if you keep looking behind you with no attention to what's ahead.

Discipline keeps us moving in the right direction even when it feels like we're stuck. But through the painful parts of your business growing pains, with discipline on your side, you'll keep driving forward to your destination without a crash. Now begs the question, how do you get to this level of discipline? Routine.

ROUTINE IS NOT YOUR ENEMY

"Gemma, I don't want to do the same thing every day."

"I can't eat the same food every day. It has to be different."

"I'll lose my freedom if I have to create a routine."

Blah, blah and blah. Are you running a business or listening to the toddler in your head?

My cat wanders into my office daily at around 4:30 pm and sits on my keyboard. When I open the blinds in my bedroom, she runs upstairs and anytime she walks inside, she headbutts my foot on the way in.

You're no different to my cat.

You may think you hate routine, but you are a routine. Most of what you do, think and say is habitual, and it's habitual because you did it repeatedly until your brain stopped thinking about it, so it can automatically just do it. Having a routine is human nature, but forming one in your business is challenging because it goes against your current one – the toddler yelling at you like above. Once you find what works for you, routine tasks require no thought, which means our brain is open to doing other valuable things like coming up with ideas, devising strategies and being creative. So you can stop shrilling at the word 'routine' because it frees your mind.

Have you ever driven to work on the same old commuting route where your mind was busy thinking about other things until you parked the car and wondered how the hell you even got there?

Hello, routine! Imagine tasks being so autopilot in your business you're running on an automatic mode the same as above. It may not feel like autopilot because it involves more thought than driving, but routine is the key to opening up more time and getting more stuff done.

If you've ever wanted to get stronger, would you go to the gym and stare at the weights expecting to get stronger and build muscle? I mean, kind of ... But no, you'd pick them up and do the same exercise in repeated reps to build strength in the same muscle group to get stronger. Think of creating a business routine as building your business muscles. You are getting stronger (getting shit done) by repetition (opening up more time) and increasing strength (growing your business.)

CONSISTENCY IS KEY

In the last chapter, you read the tale of webinars to no one, so it's no surprise consistency in business is critical. When you're running webinars to no one, consistency helps you keep doing them each time until you've improved your marketing messaging and people show up. But it's not just trialling your lead magnets. I'm talking about consistency everywhere. Whether you're consistently releasing your blog, newsletter or podcast, you always show up on social media and reply to emails.

Consistency builds trust with yourself and your clients plus helps maintain your efficiency. It enables you to keep on track with your plans, *why*, mission, vision and goals. Conversely, being inconsistent and changing things creates confusion for yourself and your audience. To ensure happy clients maintain consistency.

Let's say you commit to a weekly email newsletter. You do it for four weeks and then don't send another for three months. It looks inconsistent if you've got clients waiting for the next one. Consistency is better than random actions.

Consistency aligns with your purpose

Taking consistent steps and completing tasks in your business moves you towards your goal. If you do one task every day, it takes you forward, no matter what. Many clients ask me how long consistent action will take until they hit their business goals, but there is no answer. I'm sorry. Because every business and person is different, no one size fits exists. But consistent actions moves you forward in your business no matter what.

Consistency is how you plan, not what you plan, and using

discipline to follow through. After a while of being consistent, it forms a habit and builds a solid foundation for your business's long-term success and growth. Not to mention your own as well.

CREATING BUSINESS HABITS

You do habitual actions without thinking about it, like driving. Driving involves a bunch of activities in your brain telling your body to drive even when you're barely awake.

Thanks, brain, what a legend!

If you want to identify your current habits, think about tasks you do and how it would feel strange NOT to do them. What's the first thing you do when you get out of bed? Brush your teeth? Make coffee? Whatever it is, try not to do it tomorrow morning and see how weird that feels. Pour a glass of water with your non-dominant hand. These are all habits.

I want you to think about one thing you keep putting off doing in your business and write it below.

You will conquer it by forming a habit using the three superpowers from this chapter. But before we do that, I want to truth bomb you with what it's like to develop new habits.

It's uncomfortable.

It takes effort.

Routine is an essential part. (Just to remind you because I can hear you being a toddler.)

It takes time.

You won't know how much time until you keep doing it.

Did that answer all your questions?

I know you've got one more ... Where the hell is the good part of this?

There is excellent news, I promise. To repeat the start of this chapter, once something is a habit, it puts annoying and tedious business tasks on autopilot. So, you get them done, and you can focus on growing your business.

Now that you understand the importance of discipline, routine and consistency, let's look at how to do this.

Take the 21-day business writing challenge to practise forming a habit.

I've shared this with many clients in coaching and workshops to help them develop discipline, consistency and form copywriting as a habit. It's a fab challenge because copywriting is an essential part of business as it connects you with new clients, among other awesome things. Many of my clients tell me that it made writing fun and reduced their overwhelm.

- Step 1. Commit to 21 days.

- Step 2. Write at the same time every day.

- Step 3. Allocate ten minutes (timed).

- Step 4. Answer the same question for seven days in a row.

When it comes to Step 3, I want you to set a timer so you're not distracted by checking for when the ten minutes will be up. And when you're writing, don't overthink it. Write or type answers to the three questions I'll give you below. Sometimes you may have entire pages and sometimes a few words on a page. It doesn't matter, but please commit to the 21 days.

- Week 1. Question 1 – What are my clients' problems?

- Week 2. Question 2 – How do I help my clients?

- Week 3. Question 3 – After working with me, what's different in my client's life when they solve their problems?

I want you to enjoy this challenge. After you finish, you will have more pages and content you can repurpose in the next chapter.

Winning.

Will it be a habit after 21 days? It may, but it may not yet, but you're closer to creating awesome copy with content sitting there waiting to be repurposed and breaking the habit of copywriter's block. Speaking of repurposing, you can also use this method to develop other practices in your business.

PLAN, PLAN AND STICK TO THE PLAN

Discipline is your friend, and routine is the key to getting there. This means that planning is the key to creating a routine in your business. Why do all of this? Because consistency is helpful for your clients and you'll form good habits for yourself. Here's how to plan the shit out of yourself and into a routine.

Step 1. Decide

This may seem strange, but deciding what you want to do is critical to your success in creating a routine. Write a list of everything you want to do in your business, such as recording and scheduling your podcast, a weekly email newsletter or even a blog.

Step 2. Choose

You can list them in order of importance or just choose ONE business task you want to make into a routine. Then choose the frequency with which you're going to do this task, how long it will take you and then select the day and time. For example, one newsletter to your email list to be released on Thursday mornings and written each Wednesday at 2 pm, giving yourself an hour to write, proofread, schedule and grab snippets for repurposing on your social media platforms.

Step 3. Do

The best way to practise creating this task into a routine is to do it no matter what, even when you don't feel like it. Honour yourself, say no and know your distraction obstacles. Maintain your discipline as you build your routine muscle, and remember to give yourself a little reward afterwards.

HOW TO STICK TO YOUR ROUTINES

Building from the steps above, the key to sticking to routines is to know the amount of time you set for the task, plan it and then schedule it. Don't leave words on a to-do list flapping around on a little strip of paper, looking meaningless and easy to lose.

If you're having the 'I can't schedule my time' freakout, I get it because most of my clients shrill when I tell them to schedule the time. They prefer the easy-to-lose to-do list. Like many entrepreneurs, you're happy to plan but reluctant to plan to do it. The freak out happens when I want clients to ditch (oh, no!) the to-do list. And put the tasks on a reliable (preferably digital) calendar at a set time. A notification will pop up (the only one you're allowed to have ... remember Chapter 6) and tell you it's the time to do the thing.

Now, scheduling looks different for everyone, but please put it in a calendar, diary or whiteboard on the wall. Whichever is your preferred method, but not one that's easily lost. I want you to schedule your time to get tasks done using a kind of in-your-face method ... which one you select is up to you.

Planning what to do (before it goes into your calendar) also looks different for everyone. I plan my week ahead every Sunday night and put all business tasks for the week into my Google Calendar, so Google tells me what to do during my working hours. But trial what type of planning works better for you. Plan the night before or the month before. It's up to you.

If you're worried planning takes too long (the number one moan and groan I hear), it doesn't. It saves you time. Once you've decided everything you'll do in your business for the week (or day or month) and then add the tasks to allocated times, once that day and time arrive, you know what you're doing without wasting time thinking about what to do. Plus, this book has given you many tips and tricks on doing things when you don't feel like doing them.

In my experience, the biggest time waster for most entrepreneurs is thinking about what to do. If you've taken the time to plan everything you want to get done based on your working hours and goals, then all you have to do after that is show up and do it.

As I've said numerous times, scheduling is different for every entrepreneur. To figure out how it will best work for you, conduct a SWTS analysis on yourself – my adaptation of a SWOT analysis.

Strengths – What comes easy for you to do in your business?

Weaknesses – What's more challenging?

Threats – What gets in the way of you sticking to your

schedule and planning your day around this?

Strategies – Strategies to overcome your threats.

HOW TO BE CONSISTENT

Finally, if you're struggling with consistency, use the above methods to help you because building your discipline muscle enables you to become consistent. It's easier to be consistent when you have routines in place because you skip the wasted hours of being erratic or faffing around trying to figure out what to do next. Consistency also means opening yourself up to being bored. Most people hate consistency because they always want to do something different and get bored of the same thing, but doing the same thing repeatedly will pay off in dividends in your business.

These three tools you learnt in this chapter will help you in Chapter 9 (and everywhere) as I take you through the most challenging business barrier for most entrepreneurs to conquer – showing up on social media.

CHAPTER NINE

THE SOCIAL MEDIA HUMP

For many entrepreneurs the giant first hurdle to move past is posting on social media. Or, that you're not posting on social media to be more precise.

In this chapter I'm talking about a social media mindset that as an entrepreneur is beneficial to form so you get comfortable with being seen on the platforms and you can be in a helpful headspace about posting content. Then I'm going to show you how to develop the content. Plus, I'll teach you posting with the best ways to get content out using crafty software that lets you set and forget.

I have client after client freak out about being on social media, with some who want to avoid it completely. But the reality is it's a large part of getting yourself and your business out there for people to see you.

I tell all my clients that a website is the heart of your business, but social media is a way where you can connect with your clients in real time, give them advice and show them who you are. Without having social media as part of your content marketing strategy you risk missing out on new eyeballs to your business. People turn to social media to see if you're a 'real' business and human. Ironically many humans on social media aren't real, however, showing up as you the actual human is part of running a business.

This chapter will help you shift the social media mindset many entrepreneurs have that leads to avoiding or putting it off. If you're reading this thinking you want to close the book and keep ignoring social media, then I wrote this chapter for you.

DEVELOP A SOCIAL MEDIA MINDSET

A social media mindset is one that lets you post freely without worrying about what others think of you. The primary reason that entrepreneurs run a mile from social media, or don't act like themselves there, is because they're scared of people seeing them, which could lead to something else they fear: people that see them judging them.

A social media mindset is being so aligned with your business purpose that you'll comfortably post your messages on your social media platforms, believing that they'll help you connect with and assist your target audience regardless of any negativity you may get back. It's worth getting your message out there no matter what.

This is the social media mindset of an entrepreneur. If you're not there yet, do these sound familiar to you?

I don't want people to see me.

What if I look stupid?

People will judge me.

I can't talk about things in front of my family who follow me.

I don't know what to say.

What I've got to say isn't important.

If so, these thoughts contribute to what I call an anti-social media mindset. For those with an anti-social media mindset, the above thoughts running through your head are the most common objections I hear to posting on social media. And perhaps you've got your own restricting thoughts as well.

These are the thoughts that lead you to hide and avoid social media. This mindset isn't helpful to your business because social media, regardless of whether you like it or not, is a crucial part of business content marketing.

Now, look at these thoughts again and answer them with social media mindset thoughts.

Anti-social media mindset	Social media mindset
I don't want people to see me.	People need to see me otherwise I can't help them.
What if I look stupid?	I don't care if I look stupid.
People will judge me.	People can think what they like about me. People will always judge me and those who do aren't my clients.
I can't talk about things in front of my family who follow me.	Let my family see how much I love my business.
I don't know what to say.	I'll always find something helpful to say.
What I've got to say isn't important.	If I can help one person, what I say matters.

Having a social media mindset means showing up at least daily on social media platforms to share your message and yourself regardless of how you're feeling. Social media puts you in the public eye of the internet for anyone to find you, so it makes sense many entrepreneurs want to avoid it. But adopting a social media mindset like the one in the right column means that even though you may want to avoid posting, you'll do it anyway because it takes you in the right direction towards your business goals and vision.

Remember, you won't like all parts of your business, but as entrepreneurs we put our big human pants on. Using what you've learnt in this book so far, you've got all the tools to help you develop a social media mindset.

Part of your social hurdle is your mind freaking out about every human in the world looking at you or the complete opposite and not a single human at all. Which brings us to the step you can take to uncover your social media mindset and help you get over the hurdles.

Write down your social media concerns.

For example, why are you avoiding posting on social media?

Or why aren't you doing a live video, making reels or posting images of yourself?

Once you've uncovered your answers, pay attention to the language you use. If you see the words, *people*, *no one* and *everyone*, highlight them. As a word nerd and lover of words, I believe one word can make all the difference in a sentence, especially the sentences that run through your mind. When we think sentences like 'People will judge me', we're making broad sweeping statements that all the people will judge us, making us feel terrified, quivering at the knees that we'll be embarrassed, judged and criticised. And when we use words like, 'No one cares what I have to say', it brings out emotions such as isolation, doubt or sadness.

As you can see, this mindset doesn't help your business, and it's no wonder you want to avoid social media entirely. Is it all the people and everyone in the world? Is it no one? The answer to these questions is most likely no, so highlight and take the dramatic words out of what you're thinking because it makes posting on social media far less scary.

When you're feeling resistance against posting on social media, remember to write down what you're thinking to bring it into your awareness so you can see if it's a genuine fear or if it's your dramatic brain being a pain in the ass. Then you can refute your mind by writing or thinking something that will remind you of your social media mindset to help you connect with your *why* so you can continue posting content.

Focus on your clients

Social media isn't about you, your social media strategy is for your clients and potential clients. Taking yourself out of the picture and remembering that it's about your business and other humans will help you shift past the social media hurdle.

To help you focus on social media being about your clients, answer these three questions:

1. What do your potential clients need to hear?

2. How can you help them?

3. What will they miss out on if you don't post?

If your anti-social media mindset is preventing you from posting, answering these questions helps reconnect you with your clients and refocus social media towards being about them and not you. If you're struggling to answer the questions above, then add the word 'today' to the end of each question. This helps to make answering the questions less daunting if you focus on one day. For example, what do your potential clients need to hear from you today?

Answer this and not only are you helping shift your anti-social media mindset but you will also have authentic content done and ready to post.

Plan and streamline it

You know how important planning is when it comes to business so don't make the mistake of being on social media without a plan because posting aimlessly is useless. You can add this to the social media section of your business plan (I kept it separate for the sake of this chapter), or you can have the plan in a different document, it's up to you.

The first part of your plan is to establish your social media *why*. This is your reason for using social media as part of your content strategy and what you want to get out of it. What do you want to gain? And what is your desired outcome?

Here are some examples of social media *whys*:

- Increase followers

- Build trust

- Reach more unique people

- Develop online relationships

- Gain authority

- Get new clients

- Sell your new course

- Grow your email list.

If you're thinking, *How do you create a plan from a* why*?*, well here's how it goes. If your reason for a social media strategy is to increase your email list, then you've got a way of planning, executing and evaluating the outcomes during and after the duration of the strategy.

If your email list increases, you can check analytics for data such as which visitors clicked on your sign-up page on your website or social media platforms.

Once you've moved past the initial hurdle of avoidance it's easy to get distracted by social media and focus on aspects like pretty pictures and perfect videos. Focusing on these unimportant areas of social media is a procrastination technique, so remember your goals and purpose of posting, so you don't lose focus on your social media *why*.

Once you establish you're *why* to set goals, it's harder to lose focus and you will have something to evaluate. Ensure the goal is measurable. I've spoken about measurable goals before, so when setting the goal, ask yourself, how will I measure the result of my why? For example, if you want new followers or subscribers to your email list, then distinguish how many. If your reason is to build trust or gain authority, how will you measure this? Perhaps x amount of businesses reach out to you wanting to collaborate on a project or be a guest on your podcast. Whichever you decide, make sure the goals are ones you can measure so you'll be able to evaluate at the end of your strategy period for improvements and adjustments for your next six months.

Constrain your platforms

Before you go planning your *why* and creating goals for your socials, if you're on every social media platform, I want you to delete half of them now because you cannot commit to them all, select two or three at the most.

Select your social media platforms based on where your potential clients spend their time, not where you like to spend it. Remember to focus on your clients. You can find reports with analytical data that will help you select your platforms. You'll get demographic information such as age, gender and occupation of the people using particular social platform. Do your own research too so you can gather more in-depth physiographic information like their interests, values and opinions around social media. You can ask your current clients for information about which social media platforms they hang out on, and you can use the following questions:

- Which social platforms do you use?

- What time of day do you enjoy scrolling?

- What Facebook groups do you belong to?

- What's your favourite type of content?

- What pages do you like?

- Who do you follow on Instagram?

These questions will give you helpful information for posting and scheduling content when it comes time.

Keep your social messaging simple

Once you've selected your social media platforms, it's time to add your messaging to your plan, including what you will post. I've got two helpful methods for you to create content and get clear in your messaging.

In Chapter 1, I asked these questions:

- What are three things you wish your target audience knew?

- What are three things you hate that other people are doing in your industry?

If you skipped to this chapter first or missed Chapter 1, you can head back there and get up to speed. Now we're talking about social media. I'm adding one more question below.

- What are the three things you want to be known for?

When you've got all the answers to these questions, you have nine things about you and your niche you can repeat over and over again on social media. These become your social media messaging strategy.

Further to these messaging questions, here are more questions that will help you build content:

- What are your client's problems?

- What upsets them?

- What can't they conquer?

- What's one thing they must know?

If you can answer each question with three answers, you've got another twelve content ideas you can use, and they can also become a part of your messaging strategy.

Simple is best on social media, and repetition is also crucial because when you've got algorithms doing their thing, you never know who has seen your post and when, so don't be afraid of repetition. Re-use and repurpose your twenty-one messages using different copy, images and videos so it stays fresh but relays the same message.

The biggest question I get asked is, 'What type of post do I share?' and here is the equation I've always used:

- 60% value

- 30% connection

- 10% sales

Let's say you post five days a week, using my equation, you could post:

- 3 x value (information) posts

- 2 x connection posts (stuff you do and stuff about you)

The next week:

- 2 x value

- 2 x connection

- 1 x sales

It doesn't have to be exact, but based on the above messaging, give helpful advice, connect with your audience to display the authentic you and add in a sales post here and there, unless you have a launch or business event coming up and then you can post more about those in the lead up. There is no golden rule but remember, people use social media to be social (or waste time), not to get bombarded with sales posts.

Value post ideas

- Educational posts

- Quotes

- Share a helpful podcast

- Snippets from your podcast

- Motivational content

- Snippets from your blog

- 'How to' posts

- Q and A post with another industry expert

- Things you've learnt

- Helpful advice

- Tips and tricks

- Short case study

- Things you've learnt from your clients

- Client testimonial

Connection post ideas

- Did you know [this thing] about me?

- I discovered that ....

- My morning routine ....

- The biggest lesson I learnt from [movie/book/ person]

- This quote is stuck in my head. Here's why.............

- Three things I do to help get me through [challenging thing]

- Behind the scenes of my business

- Here's what I learnt about life from [insert pet's name]

- Why I became a ....

- One thing I'll never do again ....

- I stuffed [the thing] up, here's what I learnt

- My cat's a dickhead because ....

Posts to get comments and conversation

- Cats or dogs?

- Morning or night person?

- Summer or winter?

- Sweet or savoury?

- Tea or coffee?

- Beach or mountains?

How to write it

Stick to a simple 3-step plan when writing the copy for your social media images, videos and any shared content.

The plan is Feel, Know, Do. You may be familiar with it from my first book, *Done with dull*.

- What do I want my reader to feel?

- What do I want them to know?

- What do I want them to do?

Each post is about one thing and one action.

Let's take the 'My cat's a dickhead because' connection post.

1. I want my reader to feel amused.

2. I want them to know that my cat thinks she's a kangaroo.

3. I want them to comment below if their cat does the same thing.

These three steps create a mini plan for each social media post you write, which makes it easier for you to write and always finish each post with a mini call to action. Social media calls to action are a combination of 'follow me', 'share with a friend', 'comment below', 'tag a friend' or 'go to the link in the bio'.

Here is an example of how you could plan a post:

> Picture: My cat is asleep on my laptop with my calendar open on the screen.
>
> Copy: What's your biggest planning problem? This one is a massive hindrance for me ... Planning saves you time, stress and energy in the long run. But sometimes things get in the way ...
>
> CTA: When it comes to planning, what

gets in your way? Tell me below.

Keep it social

People aimlessly scroll through social news feeds for hours, which means you have a couple of seconds to catch their eye and stop them from scrolling past you, which means the first sentence of your copy matters. You want to hook them in and spark their curiosity, so they click on the rest of your copy to read your whole post.

Start your post with a super bold statement or attention-grabbing headline:

- You're not alone

- [Number of people] can't be wrong

- [Number] disgusting facts about [product/service]

- Here's the sickening truth about [thing]

- Uh oh! This [thing] happened

- [Product/service] is dead

- I hate to say it but ...

Ask a question because it's human nature to want to

respond with an answer, so this is another excellent way of stopping the scroll. So, if you're not feeling like a super creative word genius, use a question because it may entice your scroller to hit 'more' and read the rest of your post. Questions could be like these:

- Ever wish ....?

- Struggling to ....?

- Sick of ....?

- WTF is this?

- How can [this thing] be happening?

- Did you know that [thing]?

- Do you agree?

- What do you think?

- Which do you prefer?

- How often do you [thing]?

- Can you relate?

Social media isn't as terrifying as it seems and is an excellent marketing strategy for your business. If you want to run your business your way, be authentic and work with the clients you want to work with, then making it over the social media hump is critical because your next best client is out there waiting for you to find and speak to them.

Batch the hell out of it

Now you've made your plan, created content ideas and then written them, it's time to look at scheduling and posting.

If there's one message you take from this chapter, do not post daily yourself. Don't try to come up with fresh ideas for posts, copy and videos every day. Write them ahead of time and schedule them. Various software programs help you schedule your content for at least a month at a time. Some social media scheduling platforms include:

- Later

- Planoly

- Hootsuite

- Buffer

Plan for three or six months so you can create and prepare it ahead of time each month. Schedule a large chunk of time once a month, like four hours, or trial what works best for you, so you can create and upload the images and videos, write your copy and schedule them for the days they'll post throughout the month.

I bet you're thinking, *What if I have a fantastic idea one day for a video that I haven't scheduled?*

Make it and post it. And add in a random photo of what you did on the weekend, something silly, or of your cat being weird again. But the bulk of your strategy is a set, forget and auto-post situation. Planning your content strategy this way also helps you to design and schedule your launches, webinars or anything you're inviting people to.

Don't forget to check

I'm an avid supporter of schedule and forget, but don't forget to check. Remembering the time your scheduled post goes live on your social media platforms is critical to the success of your posts. You can go to the post and if there are comments reply and do it within the first hour of the post going live. End your reply with a question to entice a different response and conversation. Posts with high engagement do well on social media platforms and the algorithms will push your posts out to more news feeds and eyeballs.

Batching also helps with specific hashtag days, such as

#worldwineday. I use this hashtag and create a post around it because it goes with the theme of my podcast *Work Wife Wine Time*.

Jump over to Google, grab a content calendar and mark out all the days that suit your business. World Doughnut Day, World Turtle Day or International Women's Day. These days add variety to your social media marketing plan and open your posts up to additional eyeballs.

Refresher (What the hell did she say again?)

- Mindset

- Plan

- Write

- Batch

These are the four steps to making it over the social media hump to post regularly on your selected social platforms and create awareness around what thoughts are keeping you in an anti-social media mindset so you can rebut them and work your way towards a social media mindset.

Social media is an excellent way to have your business seen by many new humans and to get new clients. As an entrepreneurial human, you're here because you want your business to flourish and grow. Using social media for good and not procrastination is an excellent way to grow your business.

CONCLUSION

You've learnt what it takes to run an online solo business without your mind getting in your way, and actionable steps you can adopt that contribute to getting through the tough times in business.

Are you ready to get going with your business and be in control of what happens next? Bravo. It all starts with your thinking because without your mind on your side, your business suffers.

The cycle of business life

You learnt about how business goes around in a cycle. Your working life will feel more manageable and less resistant if you keep in control of your business mindset and embrace uncomfortable feelings. The world is binary, which means we can't know one thing without the other. You need to feel pain in business and life to get to pleasure. Once you do this, you'll create different outcomes in your business and run a business you love.

You're done with dull and are ready for head-turning, but before you can turn other heads, you must turn your own.

Don't do what you learnt in this book all in one go because it'll get overwhelming and you may get into a consumption and confusion spiral. Oh, oh! Please remember to read and action right away and use the parts that are useful to you when needed.

Embrace the discomfort of not procrastinating and break the habit of not pushing through your business fears. Think about thoughts, emotions, fear and your business stalling techniques plus all the learnings in this book at your own pace. Take a small step every day towards feeling unstuck and growing your business.

How can you do this? Simple.

Schedule 20 minutes each work day to answer this question: what am I putting off today and why? Write your answer freely, uncover what you're putting off and then open up the time to do it. Perhaps it's too much to do that day or the next, so ask yourself, what's one thing I can do that will take me one step closer to achieving this? And do that one small task.

If you can't find the time for this 20-minute exercise, think about why you can't. Is it because you're feeling uncomfortable or scared? If the answer is yes, then you know what to do, feel terrified and do it. You've got the tools to make it happen. Feel the pain to get the pleasure.

Feeling uncomfortable is the key to getting unstuck in your business and running a sustainable business your way. You've got this.

CONNECT WITH ME

I want to support you on your journey towards running your business your way so you don't feel like giving up and hiding anymore. Be a part of a worldwide shift away from being an employed human and making self-employment work for you.

Connect with me if you need coaching help to achieve all the goals you set in this book or to help you write copy. Perhaps you want to do yoga? I can help you with that as well. You can find me blabbering on Instagram, Facebook or on my website, contentlydriven.com.

What now?

I wish all entrepreneurs to embrace discomfort, understand their thinking and push through the pain barrier to get to the sweet spot of continuum. Do this so you can run your business and feel a sense of freedom to be able to share your greatness with the world.

ACKNOWLEDGMENTS

How on earth did I find myself dizzy and alone, having just moved into a one-bedroom shack with see-through curtains and no glass in the windows on the Galapagos Island of Santa Cruz? Oh yeah, I'd taken a way-too-strong-for-my-tiny-body seasickness tablet by recommendation to get to my volunteer teaching job. But not before enduring a two-hour boat ride without spewing the entire time like the 19 others on board to fulfil my dream of visiting the Galapagos Islands to hang out with giant tortoises.

I believe that whatever you put your mind to, you can achieve. I urge everyone to pursue their dreams even if no one supports them. Don't let anyone tell you something isn't possible because the human will always prevails. You may not know how to do something, but you'll figure it out on the way.

My first acknowledgment is to myself. Why? Because I've never taken the time to thank myself for having my own back. I've always believed that I can do anything, which helped me achieve so much. I thank myself for listening to the niggling voice in the back of my head (me) who always believed in me. Intuition is a powerful force, and everyone has an internal voice but most turn down its volume. If something feels right, follow it no matter what.

My very first and longest friend, Ann, is another example of pursuing a dream no matter what. Her dedication and commitment to acting and believing in herself is inspirational. Thank you, Ann, for being a badass, following your dreams without initial support and for being my lifelong friend.

To my friend Janelle who showed me what it means to be loved unconditionally and for getting past all the times we've stopped speaking for reasons we can't remember.

To my friend Mia who was my inspiration for starting my business, without whom I may never have done it. She helped me make it all happen at the beginning and showed me it's possible to work, travel and design life your way.

Finally, I am deeply grateful to those whom, because of my business, I met. They've supported (and still support) various stages of my business and its functionality, and I am lucky enough now to call my friends and advocates. Mikala, Dora, Natalie, Anna, Ashley, Lisa and Igor.

www.ingramcontent.com/pod-product-compliance
Lightning Source LLC
Chambersburg PA
CBHW071210210326
41597CB00016B/1755